(re)Discover the Joy of Creative Writing

Overcome writer's block. Boost your creativity.
Reignite your creative fuse.

Paul Lima

published by
Paul Lima Presents
www.PaulLima.com/books

(re)Discover the Joy of Creative Writing. Copyright © 2009 by Paul Lima
Cover design and book layout by Lorina Stephens. Copyright © 2009 by Lorina Stephens. www.5rivers.org
Cover photo by Kyah Green, Copyright © 2009 by Kyah Green

Published by Paul Lima Presents www.PaulLima.com/books
Manufactured in the U.S.A.
Published in Canada

All rights reserved. No part of this publication may be reproduced, stored in or introduced into a retrieval system, or transmitted in any form or by any means (electronic, mechanical, photocopying, recording or otherwise), without the prior written permission of both the copyright owner(s) and the above publisher of the book.

First Edition

Library & Archives Canada/Bibliothèque & Archives Canada Data Main entry under title:

(re)Discover the Joy of Creative Writing © 2009 by Paul Lima
Lima, Paul

ISBN 978-0-9809869-1-4

    1.   Title

Also by Paul Lima

How to Write a Non-fiction Book in 60 Days
Everything You Wanted to Know about Freelance Writing…
The Six-Figure Freelancer: How to Find, Price and Manage Corporate Writing Assignments
Business of Freelance Writing: How to Develop Article Ideas and Sell Them to Newspapers and Magazines
Copywriting that Works: Bright Ideas to Help You Inform, Persuade, Motivate and Sell!
Harness the Business Writing Process
How to Write Media Releases to Promote Your Business, Organization or Event
Do you Know Where Your Website Ranks? How to Optimize Your Website for the Best Possible Search Engine Results
Build a Better Business Foundation: Create a Business Vision, Write a Business Plan, Produce a Marketing Plan.
If You Don't Know Where You are Going, How are You Going to Get There? Business Vision Short eReport
Building Your Business Plan and Your Marketing Plan: A Step-By-Step Guide to Planning & Promoting Your Business Short eReport
Put Time on Your Side: Time Management Short eReport.

Available through www.paullima.com/books

Introduction

Welcome to *(re)Discover the Joy of Creative Writing*. This is a book for:
- would-be writers who want to explore their creative writing abilities, but may not be sure where to start;
- aspiring writers who want to develop ideas for short stories, novels or poems or have ideas but need to put flesh on the bones;
- more experienced writers and authors who want to go hunting for something new using creative writing exercises that will allow them to explore new ideas, topics and subjects.

This book is for you if you:
- are looking to plunge into the world of creative writing;
- are looking to overcome writer's block;
- are looking to boost your creativity or reignite your creative fuse;
- want to develop new ideas for stories and poems;
- have story ideas but want to expand upon them;
- want to find time, or make time, to write;
- have time to write but are not sure how to use your time productively and creatively.

(re)Discover the Joy of Creative Writing will spark ideas, get you writing and keep you writing. It will help you discover, or rediscover, the joy of writing. It will let you have fun but also encourage you to push your writing to the point where you can think seriously about completing longer works of fiction, a series of thematically-related short stories or perhaps a collection of poetry.

Unlike many books on writing, this book makes no outlandish promises of riches or mega-success, other than to say that if you work in a dedicated and disciplined manner at the exercises presented here, you will write. You may even surprise yourself with what you write and how much you write.

Creative writing (primarily the writing of fiction and poetry) is a lucrative business for some writers, certainly not all writers. While most writers aspire to fame, recognition and riches, many are happy to practice their art or engage in the craft of writing because it can be personally rewarding—even though it can be frustrating at times too. Yes, writing can lead to publishing success, but this is a getting started (or getting *restarted*) book—so getting started and having fun should be your focus.

In short, this book focuses on the personally rewarding aspect of creative writing. If you get something more than personal satisfaction and a feeling of creative fulfillment out of the book—and you just might—then bonus!

If you feel like you've been spinning your wheels, this book will get you grounded and focused. It will show you how to develop ideas and turn your ideas into stories or poems—all while having fun. What more can you ask for from a book called *(re)Discover the Joy of Creative Writing*?

Speaking of focus, this book focuses on the writing process as it pertains to short fiction (primarily) and poetry. However, the exercises here can be applied to novels, personal essays, memoirs and other non-fiction writing.

I hope to inspire you, to give you options to pursue and to help you create a solid foundation you can build upon (or *upon which you can build*, you might write if your internal editor is a strict disciplinarian who insists that all your work must conform to his or her standards—the standards of your grade five school teachers, perhaps).

On a personal note, if you would like to read some of my short fiction and poetry, feel free to visit my creative writing web index—www.paullima.com/cw.

Caveat: I've had two professional writers sweep the book for bugs (typos and grammatical errors). However, I find one or two always elude me. If you spot any errors—other than sentence fragments or sentences that start with "but" or "and", feel free to email info@paullima.com and let me know! Also, if you have any other comments on the book, feel free to email them to me.

All the best with your writing.

Paul Lima
www.paullima.com

Contents

Chapter 1: Face the Blank Page 1
Chapter 2: Directed Freefall 8
Chapter 3: Clustering (Word Association) 12
Chapter 4: Why Change? 19
    The Delta Factor 20
    The Editor's Job 23
Chapter 5: Journey through Childhood I 24
    Emotions of Childhood 26
    Journey through Childhood Exercises 26
Chapter 6: Journey through Childhood II 31
Chapter 7: Cheese Sandwiches and Motivation 35
    What Motivates You? 36
    Motivation and *What If?* 37
Chapter 8: Modelling to Write 44
    Modelling Overview 44
    Five Modelling Exercises 45
Chapter 9: The Conquest of Kong 53
Chapter 10: The Elements of Prose 60
    The Elements of Writing 60
    The Elements of Fiction 61
Chapter 11: The Characters of Fiction 69
Chapter 12: Show vs. Tell 75
Chapter 13: Elements of Poetry 78
Chapter 14: Critiquing and Editing 84
    Five Editor's Chores 87
    I.C.E.: The Cold Way to Edit 90
Chapter 15: Leading Up to Something 93
Chapter 16: Thoughts on Marketing 98
Chapter 17: Bonus Exercises 103
Chapter 18: Sentences and Paragraphs 105
Chapter 19: A Tale of Self-Publishing 111

Chapter 1: Face the Blank Page

Getting Started

So let's get started. This chapter will introduce you to the writer's journal, the writing process and Freefall (stream of consciousness)—a writing exercise to help you face the blank page and overcome any of your inhibitions when you do so. In addition, it will help you separate your creative self from your internal editor. More—much more—on how to do that, and the importance of doing it, later. First, a few...

Words for Thought

If you are just starting to write or coming back to it after a leave of absence, or if you have always written and hope to do something more with your writing, you might find of interest the following words from Diane Baker Mason, author of *Last Summer At Barebones* and several other novels:

> *There was a time when I suffered from writer's block. I didn't write for many years after my teens. I always wanted to write, but it was scary. After years and years of not writing, I thought that if I couldn't be another T.S. Eliot, there was no point in writing. I was wrong. If there is any advice I can offer writers, it is this: enjoy writing, don't give up and don't get your knickers in a knot. There will be times when you will just hate it.*
>
> *I owe much of my success to Atkinson College English professor Stanley Fefferman. When I first went to his class, I thought, he's going to teach me how to write a short story. What he told me instead was to put a pen on the paper and just write. He made it feel like such an ordinary and gentle process.*

And that is what writing can and should be—a gentle process. Diane published her first novel, *Last Summer At Barebones*, in 2001 at the age of 42. You can read more about her and her novel online at www.dianebakermason.com.

(re)Discover the Joy of Creative Writing

Writer's Journal

Since you will be writing, I suggest you start a writer's journal, using either a notebook or a specific file on your computer. Whatever the case, it should be easily accessible. Your writer's journal is where you write notes, observations and reactions as you go through this book. It will also be the place where you do your *journal exercises*. It is your safe place to write. It is not a diary. It is you engaged in the creative process, warts and all. It is you playing in your create sandbox—all on your own. It is not for public consumption. So have fun in your journal, and don't censor yourself.

Does that mean anything goes in your writer's journal? To answer succinctly: yes! Why not? It is *for your eyes only*. Enough said.

In addition, try to write in it for 15 or more minutes a day at least three days per week. Simply use what you learn—particularly Freefall and Clustering—to write on a regular basis in your journal.

Why write regularly in your journal? Making writing part of your daily routine will improve your ability to write. It will also help you establish the discipline that is required if you are to continue to write once you finish reading this book.

When is the best time to write in your journal? Whenever you can! Perhaps you can take time the first thing in the morning or just before going to bed, or instead of watching the news. Only you can find, or make, time to write.

Having a set time to write will help establish discipline, which is important if you want to tackle a larger project after you finish reading this book. In addition, over time you may find that particular themes, ideas, settings, situations or characters appear repeatedly in your journal. These recurring themes or images may become the bones over which you layer the flesh of poetry, short stories, a novel, essays, columns or articles. And that is probably the best reason to keep a writer's journal.

Writing Process

Writing is a process. That is to say, you do not sit down, start to write and, presto, produce a collection of short stories or poems, or a novel. There are five stages to the writing process. Three stages are of particular importance to the creative writing process: research, creation and editing/revision.

Research: This book concentrates on internal research as a means of assisting creation. Through journal writing exercises, you will find ideas in your work, education and/or life experiences. Of course, if you are writing about a court case and you are not an experienced lawyer or judge, you will have to do "external" research as well—for example, by interviewing judges and lawyers, by visiting courtrooms or reading books on the legal system. But external research comes after you have developed ideas, created characters and assembled some semblance of plot.

Creation: This book focuses on creating without self-censorship as a means of liberating the writer or storyteller within. It presents a number of ways to overcome interference from the internal editor that holds most would-be writers back. There will be much more on this, and many exercises to get you started and to keep you going.

Editing: As the final stage in the writing process, editing is essential. Too often, however, it is applied at the research or creation stage: unsure of your ideas, you toss them without exploring them; unsure of your writing ability, you bow to your internal editor and stop creating or you fuss over the placement of a comma or semi-colon, or the spelling of Mississauga or Mississippi instead of creating. **Most people who want to write invoke their editor as they are creating and never finish a first draft.** You can be analytical and edit your work after you have completed a solid first draft. After all, the work is not going to go away. So focus on creating first and editing afterwards. There will be more on this later in the book.

To put it more succinctly, as William Forrester, a reclusive writer in the novel *Finding Forrester* (by James W. Ellison) says to his young protégé: "You write your first draft with your heart. You write your second draft with your head."

Even if I don't use those exact words again in this book, this is a recurring theme of the book.

One last word on self-censorship: while many writers start editing too early in the writing process, some writers never get to do any editing. In fact, they do very little writing. They censor their ideas before they begin to write. While there are many complex reasons for this, the exercises included in this book are here to help you create without self-censorship. Again, your writer's journal is your safe place to play with your writing. So have fun. And don't censor yourself.

Preparation and Organization

I mentioned that there were two other aspects to the writing process. They are Preparation and Organization. They are important parts of the process when you are engaged in business writing or promotional writing. However, we will take a quick look at them here.

- **Preparation:** In business writing, or if you are writing non-fiction, you want to assess your audience—their level of understanding, expectations and subject knowledge—before you start writing. You do this so you can convey information they want to know in a way they can understand.

In many ways, you might do this if you are writing genre fiction—romance or detective mysteries, for instance. Readers of genre fiction have certain expectations that you pretty much have to meet if you want them to appreciate your work—and buy your next book. In addition, part of the preparation process involves establishing your primary purpose. For the most part, you want to entertain when you are writing fiction. That does not mean you can't have a moral to your story or that you can't teach the reader something about the world around them. However, if you try to do this in a heavy-handed manner, you might put off readers—unless they tend to read fiction that has a moral to it or want to learn something when reading fiction (which is why you think about your reader expectations).

Organization: Non-fiction and business writing should unfold in a logical manner. Fiction, on the other hand, can start at the end of the story and circle back to the beginning. It can start part way through a story and reveal the past in flashback. It can jump all over and through time and space and leave the reader dazed and confused. The reader can choose to read on, or not. Some readers may like writing that flows through time and space in a linear manner; some may like writing that explodes or otherwise exploits time and space. It's all subjective. The fact is, you have to decide the approach you want to take—and sometimes you may not even know the approach you are going to take until you have engaged in creative exercises or perhaps even several drafts of a work.

Having said that, if you have a solid sense of your characters and the plot you would like to explore, or if you are writing a particular commercial genre, it might not hurt to do what many business and non-fiction writers do: prepare an outline before you start to write. By doing so, you break your document into manageable chunks. This makes it easier to stay on track while you are writing. And if you feel like going off track while writing, you can do so safe in the knowledge that you have an outline to come back to should your exploration not bear fruit.

Note: If you are interested in writing non-fiction, you might find *How to Write a Non-fiction Book in 60 Days* of interest. You can read about the book online at www.paullima.com/books. However, *this* book is about the joy of creative writing. With that in mind, let us leave the logical world of the writing process behind and get on with creating!

Creation

While we will look at specific internal research exercises that will help spark your creative side, I want to start with a couple of liberating creative writing exercises. First, a few thoughts on creation from Stephen King:

> *"Never look at a reference book while doing a first draft. You want to write a story? Fine. Put away your dictionary, your encyclopaedias, your World Almanac and your Thesaurus.... You think you might have misspelled a word? Okay, so here's your choice: either look it up in the dictionary to make sure you have it right–and break your train of thought–or spell it phonetically and correct it later. Why not? Do you think the word is going to go away? When you sit down to write, write. Don't do anything else except go to the bathroom, and only do that if it absolutely cannot be put off."*

Undirected Freefall

With King's words in mind, we are going to look at a creative writing exercise called Freefall. This particular form of Freefall is also called Undirected Freefall or Stream of Consciousness.

Freefall is a means of writing whereby you literally write without stopping for five minutes or more. Think of yourself as an artist practicing gesture sketching (rapidly drawing lines or "gestures" that do not necessarily become pictures, but enable the artist to play and experiment with lines that he or she might later incorporate in pictures).

You don't have to have anything in particular, or at all, to write about. You just put pen to paper (or fingers to keyboard) and write, write, write... You don't stop... No matter what. You tap into that thought stream that is flowing through your mind even as you are reading this (hear it rushing through your mind as you read?) and write... write... write.... If you feel yourself coming to a halt, then doodle or use ellipsis (...) until you tap back into the stream. Do not stop to correct spelling or grammar. Do not stop to reflect upon your work.

It can feel unusual to write when you think you have nothing to say, or to continue to write when you know you have made a typo or grammatical error, but that is the whole point: *To jump into the stream and let the current take you somewhere, anywhere or nowhere.*

It is a technique you should employ when keeping your journal. If you try it and stumble, get back up and carry on. It can take a bit of getting used to, writing without stopping, although you will probably take to it like a fish to water (or any other cliché you can think of when you are Freefalling and the perfect analogy does not come immediately to mind).

Journal Exercise: Undirected Freefall

What I suggest you do now is sit comfortably someplace where you will not be interrupted for the next while, and *write for five or ten minutes*…. Or until you feel you've reached the end of whatever comes out….

Simply pick up your pen or pencil (suggested/recommended) or open a new page in your word processor and start wherever you start…

And don't end until you end….

<u>If you are not ready to Freefall</u>: Go have a cup of tea, go for a stroll, go pet your dog or cat or talk to your bird… But don't put off starting for more than an hour unless you are right now going to work or to sleep, or your house is on fire.

When you are ready….

<u>Begin your Freefall….</u>

Freefall Purpose

Is there a point or purpose to Freefall? Is there a point or purpose to all the gesture sketching an artist does, the voice exercises an opera singer does, the stretching a runner does? Yes. This is your warm-up. This is you getting in shape. This is you learning to write for the sake of writing. This is you in a no-pressure, not-for-publication situation discovering the fun of writing, the love of writing. You can do this. If you don't do this, there is a chance that you will not do much writing at all.

Before you go to Chapter 2, try several more Freefalls. Try them at different times during the day or while sitting in different locations—when you are on your own and when there are people milling around. Try them when you are surrounded by silence or when there is music playing. Try them when you are feeling up, down, bored, elated. Eventually, you might settle into a *best time to Freefall* time. The important thing is that you find at least 15 to 20 minutes every day or two to Freefall in your journal. Make doing so part of your writing routine!

I want to stress here that your freefall does not have to be a straight narrative. Have fun. Play. Experiment. Push your personal boundaries. If you latch on to something that feels like a "story," run with it. But do not try to impose form or narrative on your freefall. Write fast. Do not pause. Write fast. Do not pause. There will be other exercises in this book to help you shape your Freefalls. But for now make sure you are playing with it in the privacy of your journal.

Even as you are working on other exercises in this book continue to Freefall. You never know what will come up, what you will latch on to that you can convert into... who knows what. And at this point, we don't care what. We just want to write and have a bit of fun doing it. That is all. Full stop.

So, when you are ready....

<u>Begin your second Freefall....</u>

Chapter 2: Directed Freefall

Getting Started

Do you have time to write? Time is there. It's yours to use. The question is: How do you want to use it? If you are having difficulty with time, look at what you do with your time, and see what you can cut back on, or cut out.

Instead of reading the newspaper every day, read the newspaper every second or third day. Cut out a TV program. Go to bed 20 minutes earlier than usual and use the time for writing. Wake up 20 minutes earlier than usual... You get the picture.

So, how was Freefall? Liberating or frustrating? Either way, don't be concerned. The way you feel about it can change like the weather. The important thing to do is this: Freefall in your journal on a regular basis.

You will be amazed at what comes up, the material that floats to the surface that you can later analyse and perhaps use in (or to start) stories, poems or other writing. In addition, Freefalling on a regular basis will make you a better writer. It's like working out. Makes you healthy so you are ready to run the race or lift that piano when the time comes to run the race or move the piano. Or write the short story. Or novel.

So stick with it. We use Freefall as part of other writing exercises, including...

Directed Freefall

Directed Freefall works in a manner similar to undirected Freefall, only you have a beginning—something to start the stream flowing in a particular direction. You can find Directed Freefall "beginnings" almost anywhere: a phrase on the radio, a sentence in a newspaper or book, a line from a poem, a snippet of overheard conversation....

The first line sometimes imposes structure on a narrative passage. *But not always.* Sometimes it inspires. *But not always.* Sometimes it is a relief to have somewhere to start; sometimes it feels like you are shackled.

Journal Exercise: Directed Freefall

Again, think of yourself as an artist practicing gesture sketching. Play and experiment. This time you have a first line and it may influence your first few gestures. Or not. This is Freefall. You do not have to create stories here. Just create. Once you get started, don't stop. You're off to the races and you don't stop until you collapse in an exhausted heap. When you are ready to write, write down the line below, and then....

<u>Begin your Freefall....</u>
- It took me a long time to....

When you have completed your Directed Freefall, take a short break. When you are ready, choose another line and start a five-minute Directed Freefall...
- Mimi watched as the birds...
- In the old woman's face I saw...

Write down one of the lines above and....
<u>Begin your Freefall....</u>

Freefall Regularly

So, how was the Directed Freefall? Liberating or frustrating? Different than Undirected Freefall or similar to it? Try both daily. You may determine that one works for you, the other doesn't. Or you may find it enjoyable to use Undirected Freefall in the morning when you are trying to wake up your brain or in the evening when you are trying to empty it of the stuff you stuff into your cranium during the day. You might use Directed Freefall when you feel you have a place to start or overhear a great line you cannot resist playing with or when you find a line or image in your Undirected Freefall you wish to explore further.

Play with both Directed and Undirected Freefall in your writer's journal on a regular basis. The goal is to see where they take you, to have fun, to play, to be silly or super-serious, to create for the sake of creating. To see what comes up, what develops.

As you Freefall, you may notice the appearance of certain recurring themes and images. I am not going to play pop-psychologist and tell you that your subconscious self is attempting to communicate with your conscious self. (Although that might be exactly what is happening. But I'm not going to tell you that.) Instead, allow me to say that your writing voice is trying to break through. And it is important to listen to the voice, liberate the voice, if you want to liberate your writing.

Does that mean if science fiction themes do not bubble up to the surface, you cannot write SF? Absolutely not. You can apply Freefall (and the other writing exercises in this book) to any genre. However, the way themes and images that surface in Freefall make it into your writing, no matter the genre you tackle, may surprise you. So listen to the voice. Learn how to cultivate and nurture it rather than suppress it. Enjoy where it takes you at this stage of your writing.

Does that mean you must use everything that comes up? Absolutely not. Some of it you might use, but not all of it. And that's perfectly all right. As I said earlier, writing is a process and at this point, you should be having fun creating. As you create, do not concern yourself with grammar and spelling. When you finish a Freefall, put your work away for 24 or 48 hours. When you pick it up again, look for lines, ideas, themes or characters that you find interesting/intriguing. This may be material you want to develop as you progress through the book. *Or not.*

The goal here is to plant a thousand seeds to see what blooms. That's what you cultivate—the seeds that bloom. The rest? It's creating. It's warm up. It's inventing and discovery. It's sketching. Most gesture sketches are tossed. But the artist is a better, stronger more creative artist for having done the exercises.

So try a few more Undirected and Directed Freefalls. Don't invoke your editor. Not yet. If you find something that excites you, that you want to develop, cultivate, polish... put it aside for now and carry on with the book. There will be time enough for revising and editing later on.

But hey, if something overwhelms you and you have to run with it, do so. You can always come back to the book later.

Directed Freefall Lines to Keep You Going

If you enjoyed Directed Freefall, you might appreciate the list of Directed Freefall lines (below). They are meant to get you started and keep you going with Directed Freefall. Feel free to play with them. But don't forget to search for you own beginnings as well.

Additional Directed Freefall lines:
- Looking through the scrapbook of my childhood...
- I never thought it would happen to me...
- Mimi watched as the birds...
- On the street where I grew up...
- In the old woman's face I saw...
- The last thing I remember...
- Whenever I see snow...
- "*&%$#@*^$!"
- The first time that...
- What I really wanted was...
- Nothing looked familiar to...
- I write because...
- Terry took a deep breath before...
- In a dusty box in the basement there is...
- Chris looked out the window and...
- "Yes she was pretty, but just not her face..."
- In my mother's favourite story about me...
- I resent it when...
- It was raining the day that...
- You're not going to like this, but...
- Boiling Fred's hat in the pasta sauce, Mary thought....
- An eerie mist clung to the city...
- Chris was determined to...
- I tripped, I fell, I missed the ground...
- "You're kidding? Right? You're not...."
- I felt it, a presence, behind me...
- Fifteen minutes is all I have...
- "Can you help me?" Rae asked the stranger...
- This is where it happened, officer...
- Looking back over my life, I see....
- In my mother's hands, I see...
- Terry place the flower on the casket and....
- Coming at me, the tree and the purple cow....

(re)Discover the Joy of Creative Writing

Chapter 3: Clustering (Word Association)

Getting Started

So far, we've experienced two writing exercises meant to get you started and to help you sustain your writing. Freefall is also meant to loosen you up and to help you overcome premature editing, something that plagues many writers. Freefalling regularly should help you overcome the voice of the internal censor who says spelling and grammar are paramount, which gets in the way of creativity. Spelling and grammar count, but who cares about spelling and grammar when you are having a private moment in your journal or when you are on a creative roll. The editor has his or her place, and it is not at the beginning of the writing process.

Writing is a process. Editing and revision have their places—after you have had fun inventing, conjuring, creating and playing. You don't have to buy into that philosophy, but I urge you to try to separate the creator within from the editor and see how it goes. I find it brings much more joy to my writing. In fact, I was seldom able to complete a first draft of a short story until I separated the two.

I wrote *The Conquest of Kong* (you get a copy of the short story later in the book) as a Freefall (after a series of Clustering exercises, which we are going to look at in this chapter). I had to do a lot of spit and polish on it *afterwards*, but the basic story came out in one sitting. The final version was awarded a Judge's Choice in the *Toronto Star* short story contest.

With that in mind, we are going to stick with loosening up exercises. I am going to introduce you to an internal research exercise, known as *Clustering* (also known as brainstorming, mind mapping and word association), to further spark your creativity. We are going to continue to leave the editor out of the process, for now. But before we try Clustering, how about a few...

Words for Thought

Here are a few words on writing that I'd like to share with you.

"What the writer often lacks is not ideas but a means of getting in touch with them." – Gabriele Rico

Internal research, using the techniques presented in the next couple of chapters, will enable you to get in touch with your idea seeds. Once planted, they can blossom into amazing passages of writing. Not every seed will blossom. Nor should they. Your job is to cultivate and nurture the seeds that seem healthiest.

"I never go into the writing of anything knowing how it ends, or what the ultimate fate of all these people will be. I only know I want to explore their lives in a certain context. So I get in there and start walking with them and finding out who they are ... and other things happen." – Timothy Findley

"Little children can create wonderful, uninhibited stories full of fanciful characters. But as the years pass, the regimens of school and community kill the storyteller that lives within each of us. To write fiction, you have to dig deep and discover that story-teller." – W. P. Kinsella

This is why we have to stop censoring ourselves when we create. Revision/Editing—correcting spelling, grammar, refining the plot, choosing more powerful words and developing characters more fully—occurs later, after creation. That is not to say you are doing anything wrong if you develop your characters or outline your plot before you write a story or novel. Some prolific authors will tell you to never begin anything without an outline. However, before you get to the outline stage you need to do some brainstorming.

You need to feel comfortable with letting your writing flow (a state that Freefall allows you to achieve) before you plunge into any serious creation, no matter how fully developed your characters are or how fully outlined your plot is. In other words, you have to get something down on paper before you can edit.

With that in mind, let's move on to...

Clustering

Clustering is a form of word association or brainstorming that helps you conduct what I've referred to as <u>internal research</u> before you create. It enables you to put on paper all you know about a topic and all you associate with a topic before you write. It helps you get your knowledge out in the open and lets you focus on creation by reducing the time you have to spend pondering your subject matter or imagination as you write. It also sparks writing ideas because, as you Cluster, your mind makes associations and produces images that it would have not otherwise produced. And these ideas/associations can help enrich your writing.

To Cluster, you simply write a <u>key word</u> or phrase in the middle of a page, underline it and circle it. Then draw a dash from the circle and write down the first word or phrase you associate with the <u>key word</u> and circle that new word or phrase. Then draw a dash from the new circle and write down the first word or phrase you associate with the word or phrase in the circle....

The lines and circles are meant to spark the creative side of your brain, so keep on going until you feel that the word association string has come to an end. Go back to your <u>key word</u>, draw another line from it, and write down the next word or phrase that comes to mind and carry on... Soon you will have on your page something that looks like a messy spider's web.

Keep up the Clustering process until you feel a natural end to your Cluster: you may have two strings; you may have 22 or more association strings. There is no right or wrong amount.

On the next page, you will find an example of Clustering using the key word *Clustering*.

What to Do with It?

What do you do with your Cluster? We'll let that wait until the next Chapter. For now, however, I'd like you to try another journal exercise.

Journal Exercise

Before you Cluster, read the above instructions again. Also, before you Cluster, loosen up on a scrap of paper by quickly drawing circles (or ovals) and connecting them with lines. Once you are ready, Cluster the word below.

<u>Begin your Cluster.......</u>
Key Word: to Cluster: **HEART**

(re)Discover the Joy of Creative Writing

Clustering & Freefall in Harmony

So, how was Clustering? Were you surprised by what came up? Pleased, delighted, concerned, angered? Try to Cluster other words or phrases. There are more key words in this chapter that you can use but feel free to come up with your own key words as well.

Use your writer's journal as a place to Cluster and Freefall on a regular basis. You may be amazed at what comes up—the material that floats to the surface that you can later analyse and perhaps use in stories, poems or other writing. And if you are looking for a way to use Clustering outside of creative writing, try it the next time you have to write an article, essay, memo or report. Pick a key word that relates to whatever you have to write about and Cluster. Clustering will help you get down on paper everything you associate with the topic (and then some) before you start to write. It is an excellent pre-writing exercise.

Journal Exercise

Before I tell you a few more things about your internal editor in the next chapter, I'd like you to Cluster another word. This time, I want you to try something a little different. The process is the same: Write down your key word, draw a circle around it, draw a line from it and write your next word. Circle it, draw a line...

However, when you finish your Clustering, *flip into Freefall*.

How do you know you have finished your Clustering? You will feel it. You will feel the urge to write. You will resist the urge at first, but at some point you will end your Cluster and start to Freefall....

Let the Cluster inspire your Freefall; however, continue to write without censoring yourself. You do not have to include in the Freefall all the words and phrases of you Cluster, but if you feel the Freefall slowing down, glance at your Cluster for inspiration. After all, the Cluster contains all the words and phrases you associate with the key word. And what is creative writing but a collection of words, phrases, images, metaphors (sentence, paragraphs, chapters or stanzas) associated with a central theme or plot or character types?

So, if you are ready, write down the key word below and...

<u>Begin your Cluster....</u>

Key Word: to Cluster: **HELP**

(Don't forget to *flip into Freefall* when you feel the urge to write.)

Supplementary Clustering Material

Below are a number of words you can use for Clustering. Before you move on, do try at least one or two more Cluster/Freefall combinations. Chose words from the list that resonate with you or pick your own words or phrases. Cluster your name, or your parents or other family members. Don't forget to flip into Freefall when you complete your Cluster. Add Clustering to your journaling arsenal.

Additional Clustering key words

• Letting go	• Feast
• Needles	• Going Away
• Fish	• Lilacs
• Apple	• Horse
• Christmas	• Home
• Cat	• Writing
• Dog	• Boundary
• Woods	• Knife
• Beach	• Sunset
• Vacuum	• Because
• Ouch	• Hands
• Happy	• Traffic
• Fish	• Sky
• Love	• Breakfast
• School	• Alone
• Fist fight	• Work
• Marbles	• Chocolate
• Mud	• Church
• Games	• Lover
• Skating	• Exercise
• Lost	• Trees
• Prisoner	• Sex
• Future	• Life

• Me	• Death
• Dreams	• Walk
• Friends	• Snow
• Enemy	• Ice
• Candy	• Birthday
• Puppy	• Family
• Gun	• Heaven
• Old woman	• Hell
• Escape from reality	• Heaven and Hell
• Storm warnings	• God (or your personal deity)

Additional Clustering Exercises

- Cluster each member of your family.
- Cluster each room in the house where you grew up.
- Cluster words or phrases that have meaning to you.

And don't forget to Freefall after each Cluster!

Chapter 4: Why Change?

Getting Started

Quick word about novels. A lot of the writing that this book asks you to do happens in short spurts, although many readers graduate from sprinting to marathon writing. If you have a big idea, one that suits a novel, feel free to apply the exercises to that work. But don't make that your primary or only goal. Remember, this is a *joy of writing* book meant to help you to create and to work with your internal editor in a constructive manner.

Most people who are new to writing fiction start with short stories. Short stories run from about 1,000 to 5,000 words and are complete in themselves—beginning, middle and ending or resolution. (You will learn more about the elements of fiction, applicable to short stories and the novel, in another chapter). If you aspire to write a novel, I encourage your aspirations. So, before we introduce the editor and look at other ways to work with Clustering, allow me to say a few things about the novel.

The modern novel tends to run about 350 pages with about 350 words per page. That's 122,500 words. Divide that by maybe 15 chapters and you get just over 8,000 words per chapter. (You can have more or fewer words in the novel, more or fewer words per chapter, more or fewer chapters... The main thing is that you tell the story.) Each chapter should tell a section or segment of the story. The reader should be able to shut the novel at the end of a chapter feeling as if they are closing the book on a segment of the life of the main character (protagonist).

At the same time, you want to leave the reader wanting to know what happens next. So there should be feelings of conclusion and suspense at the end of each chapter. That is what sustains the reader—the ups and downs that run through the life of the main character leading up to the climax of the book.

In many ways, it might seem like a conscious or manipulative way of writing. And it is. But the first draft can spring from Freefall. Get the story down on paper, then let your editor look at it and make conscious decisions as to how to build in some suspense, how to end a chapter leaving the reader curious about what happens next. So the same principals apply to the novel as to any act of fiction. Write the story first, edit later.

Editor Revisited

This book moves from the abstract to the concrete. The hope is that the first few chapters will allow you to loosen up and exercise your creative writing muscles. If you still feel tight, try more Clustering and Freefall. You want to get to the point where you are writing freely, without undue influence from your editor. But, as I've said, the editor is an important part of the writing process. What I hope to do through this book is introduce you to a kinder, gentler editor: one who does not interfere with the creative process but rather respects it and works with you after your initial creative endeavours.

Before we get the kinder, gentler editor to help us with the ending of our work, a reminder: **the creative portion of your writing does not end here.** Continue to Freefall and Cluster in your journal. Use these techniques to get you started, to find ideas and inspiration. Use Clustering for internal research, especially when developing ideas or characters. And rest assured that Freefall and Clustering are not the only creative exercises you will be introduced to. There will be more exercises to keep you writing.

The Delta Factor

I want you to look at several of your Cluster/Freefalls from the previous Chapter (or other Cluster/Freefalls you have done since.) Pick one or two that feel the most inspired, closest to your heart or closest to what you want to accomplish with your writing. Look at the first half a dozen sentences or the first paragraph of your Cluster-inspired Freefall. Copy the first few sentences or the first paragraph or two of your Freefall and paste this *beginning* at the *end* of the Freefall. (Or if you are using a journal, rewrite your *beginning* at the *end* of the Freefall.) All will be made clear below. For now, go with the flow.

Why am I asking you to look at where your Freefalls started and then copy and paste the beginnings at the end? Often, short stories, poems, even novels, end near to where they began. Notice I said *near*, not *in the same place*. Between the beginning and end, some movement or change occurs in the character(s) and the situation. Perhaps the main character has a better understanding of him/herself, his/her past, his/her present in relation to her past.... Whatever. The important point is this: *Change has occurred.*

I call that the *Delta Factor*. Delta (the triangle symbol) is used in mathematics to represent change. And that's what your stories need: *change*. In other words, where you end up must be different from where you began. Having said that, your story can start at the end, and then you can take the reader on a journey that shows how your story (your main character) arrived at that end. Yet somehow that end (which is where your story began) must be different than the end at the beginning—at least in the reader's mind. Otherwise, what was the journey all about? In fact, you can start anywhere and end anywhere. The important thing is that something has changed and the reader gets it (or doesn't get it—but not because there is nothing to get).

If you want to watch a movie that plays on narrative time convention (and you don't mind swearing and violence) rent *Pulp Fiction*. When you get to the end of the movie, you will realize that the movie actually ends about one-third of the way through the lives of the characters. You will see, at the end of the movie, that one character is about to change and the other one isn't (which leads to his death half way through the movie). Confusing? Not if the story is told, and structured, well.

And in the End...

But I digress. Let's get back to writing, with a Delta example. A creative writing student once submitted a Cluster-based Freefall ("woods" was the key word) that began:

> *In the woods I walk. I inhale the dampness of the earth—a peculiar, musky smell. True nature's ripe aroma. Following the trail through thick, green foliage, I see trillium flowers blooming in the shadows. Sunlight seeps through the broad branches, which shelters the flowers and damp earth. In the shadows are all these bugs. Biters. I want to commune with nature, but think I am lost. All I can do is rush headlong through the woods and swat wildly as clouds of bugs descend...*

In the Freefall, the narrator goes through a horrible time with the bugs. Gets more lost. Hears eerie sounds and fantasizes about strange creatures in the woods. She falls asleep at one point but a squirrel drops an acorn on her head, which hurts but wakes her from her reverie. Then she sees a deer and fawn in a clearing. It's a magical moment. She watches as they eat the damp foliage, then dart off. As she tries to follow them, she discovers where she is, figures out her way home and soon emerges from the woods .

The story ended there, with her emerging into the sunshine. I asked her to paste her opening paragraph on to the end, reread her story and then edit the opening that she had pasted to the end. This is how the revised story ended:

> *Out of the woods I walk, no longer stumbling through thick foliage. No longer enveloped by the scent of raw earth. The imagined sounds are already faded; the buzzing bugs barely a memory. But I carry with me my mementoes—a bump on the head from the acorn dropped by the squirrel and the vision of deer and her fawn that I will never forget.*

Notice how "out of the woods" parallels the "into the woods" opening? What she did here was more than paste the beginning at the end. She let the beginning inspire the end. She rewrote the beginning at the end and demonstrated that change had occurred—a change that reflected where the story began but was somehow different because of all that had gone on.

Do all stories or poems have to reflect their opening lines? No. Not all. But there needs to be change. Pasting your beginning at the end is one way of ensuring change happens. Sometimes when you do this, it will inspire you to edit other aspects of the story—even the beginning—so you can get to the point where you decided to end it.

I often find that when the process of pasting my beginning at the end and then revising it helps me edit my beginning. You see, once I have a better sense of where my story should end and of what change has occurred, I can then ask myself if I believe my story has started where it should have started. It's as if once I know where the story truly ends, I can discover where it should actually begin.

I hope this doesn't seem too convoluted. The fact is, any writing needs to be edited and this is one way of having your creative self work hand-in-hand with your internal editor—instead of being at odds with the editor.

It is this change (the Delta factor) that makes the story work. It is the change that makes the reader say, "I get it!" (Or sometimes, "I don't get it!") The point, theme, purpose, meaning (or "whatever") of the story (or poem) is often found in the change that takes place between the Alpha (beginning) and Omega (end).

Journal Exercise

Before you read on, find at least one Freefall (Freefall, Directed Freefall or Cluster-inspired Freefall) and paste the beginning at the end. Read what you have written again. Decide if you want to change the pasted-on ending. Or perhaps you want to change the beginning and new ending. Play with it. Not too much. Not for too long (unless you are having fun with it).

In other words, you don't have to try to turn what you've written into a fully edited short story. It may be you've written an extended anecdote, the beginning of a personal essay or simply a descriptive passage. What I want you to do is think on the opening and the ending of whatever it is you wrote, and see if you can ensure there is a Delta factor—change—between where your writing opens and where it ends.

Try this process several times, with different Freefall passages, before you move on.

The Editor's Job

As we can see, one of the editor's jobs is to ask: Does this story start where it should? (More on this in the Chapter on *Leads*.) Does it end where it should? But to do that the editor has to have some raw material to work with. The raw material is the Freefall you have created.

When reading over a first draft, the editor asks: What has happened here? What has changed during the course of the story? What hasn't changed? What could or should change. What shouldn't? Why? Why not?

It is the editor's job to look at creation analytically and to help you reach conclusions about what should or shouldn't be done with the work to move it forward and make it more complete. Yes, some editors (perhaps unruly from their banishment from the creative process) might work to sabotage you by giving you nothing but negative feedback. However, when you work in a collaborative manner with your editor, you will be able to more easily discern which of your creations you should move forward with.

Suddenly it's not such a big deal that of all the seeds you planted only two or three feel as if they are about to bloom. Sometimes you don't see the potential in your work right way. The passage of time can, at times, help you determine what will and what will not bloom.

As Natalie Goldberg, author of *Writing Down the Bones*, says:

"Every time we begin writing, we wonder how we did it before. Each time is a new journey with no maps. The best test of a piece of writing is over time. If you're not sure of something, put it away for a while. Look at it six months later. Things will be more clear."

Distance from your Freefalls can give you (in mode as editor) perspective on your writing—help you determine what stands the (short-term) test of time and is worth keeping, worth working on, worth pushing further....

If you do feel your editor sabotaging your creative efforts early on, try telling him or her or it the following: "Get thee behind me, Editor." Give your raw Freefalls the benefit of distance. Continue to work on Freefalls and Clustering until you feel your confidence in your ability to create has grown.

Later in the book, we look at working with your editor in greater detail. For now, play with some beginnings and endings, and don't let the editor intrude upon your Freefalling and Clustering/Freefalling when you are creating.

Chapter 5: Journey through Childhood I

Getting Started

Childhood is a rich source of creative ideas. After all, every character has a childhood—whether the writer delves into it or not. And every writer has a childhood, which is well worth delving into, even if—especially if—the writer delves into it and fictionalizes it. We will use a number of techniques—including Freefall and Clustering—to help us draw on childhood memories and experiences that can be used to find and explore ideas for stories and poems and to infuse writing with the power of raw emotion.

The focus will be on creation. Although you collaborated with your editor in the last chapter, remember that you brought in the editor after creating. There is no need to allow the editor to intrude here, while in creative mode. There will be time enough for editing when the creating is done.

Words for Thought

Before we begin, here are a few words that I would like to share with you:

> *"When I stated writing I started from childhood. I never write about where I am right now. It takes a while to process events and to digest them."*
> - Alice Munro

As Alice Munro indicates, writing is often based on reflection—looking back on events after you've had time to deal with them and digest their significance. Doing so makes you a better storyteller. Reflecting on childhood is also a great way to find and incorporate powerful emotions in writing. And emotions make writing come alive and ring true for others. In short, a story without emotion is like a day without sunshine: dull, flat, dreary.

That doesn't mean any reader will enjoy or relate to a story just because it packs an emotional punch. Reading, and how readers react to emotion, is a very personal and subjective experience. However, I put it to you that most readers would react with a big yawn to a story that lacked emotion.

With that in mind, here are a few more words for thought:

> I wish I had kept a diary over the years. The memory sometimes plays tricks or is forgetful, and we miss a lot of the past that could be helpful in our present.
> - Sidney Sheldon
>
> Some things you never lose no matter how long they've been gone. - Pogo
>
> Some people are ashamed of their past and others just write best sellers.
> - Anonymous
>
> It took me my whole life to learn how to paint like a child.
> - Pablo Picasso

It doesn't hurt to learn how to **create** with your heart on your sleeve, with the emotions of a child or adolescent. If it all seems too extreme, you can always pull it back when you shape your story or poem (*edit* your work). The goal now, however, is to find the things that you think you've lost (or you may have hidden or misplaced)—to connect with your past, build on it and push it somewhere strange called fiction or poetry.

Feeling a tad dubious? Read on.

Marcel Proust, the French novelist, is best known for *Á La Recherche Du Temps Perdu* (*Remembrance of Things Past*), his autobiographical novel told mostly in a stream-of-consciousness (Freefall) style. The work collected pieces from Proust's childhood, observations of high-class lifestyle, gossip and recollections of the closed world in which the author never found his place. The key scene in the novel is when a madeleine cake (a small, rich cookie-like pastry) enables the narrator to experience the past as a simultaneous part of his present existence.

> Proust writes: "And suddenly the memory revealed itself: The taste was that of the little piece of madeleine which on Sunday mornings at Combray (because on those mornings I did not go out before mass), when I went to say good morning to her in her bedroom, my aunt Léonie used to give me, dipping it first in her own cup of tea or tisane...."

If cookies and tea, and the memories associated with it, can inspire a significant novel, then it might be worth your while to journey through childhood....

Again, what we are trying to do here is to create. Drop a thousand seeds and see what is worth nurturing. Remember, at this stage *you are writing journal entries*. You are not writing for publication. So there is no need to censor or judge yourself. You are here to find memories, emotions and feelings.

Eventually, you may choose to push some of what you find into fiction. Or not. In the meantime, enjoy the writing exercises!

Emotions of Childhood

Why are childhood emotions so powerful? Childhood is where emotions are at their rawest. Notice how quickly kids are prepared to laugh, cry, scream, express frustration, boredom, anger... the whole emotional range. The objective here, as you write, is to be in touch with the full range or your emotional experiences so you can incorporate appropriate emotions in your work.

The exercises in this chapter are meant to help you recreate incidents from childhood, find emotions and images associated with them and use material you find as starting points for your writing. And if you find yourself exaggerating or telling lies creatively in your writing, no problem! With that in mind, here are writing exercises to help you find ideas and emotions that may be buried beneath the rubble of childhood. Try these exercises and see where they take you or where you go with them.

Journey through Childhood Exercises

For the purpose of the five exercises below, I define childhood as any time between birth and the age of 16. (Feel free to extend the age if appropriate.) You can write a lot this chapter, so I suggest you pace yourself. Having said that, only you can set a pace with which you are comfortable. Do not concern yourself with editing your work. As mentioned earlier, focus on creating. Put the work away as you complete it. Come back to it after you finish reading this book and let your editor help you determine if you should pursue further any of the raw work you complete here.

Exercise 1: The Possessions of Childhood

Create a list of the possessions you had as a child. List all you can remember, or focus on a particular age or age range and the possessions from that age or age range.

Choose one childhood possession from your list and Cluster it. Once you have finished your Cluster, flip into Freefall. If you wish, use some or all lines below to help write a series of short (or long!) Directed Freefalls.

- The possession I am thinking of is...
- I got it from...
- I got it when...
- And kept it for...
- I used it for...
- I kept it until...

- What it meant to me then was...
- The memories it brings back are...
- Thinking about this possession now, I feel...

Try this exercise with several other possessions from childhood. Or create a list of possessions that siblings or friends had. Pick one from your list and <u>Cluster</u> it. Once you have finished your Cluster, flip into Freefall and see where you go when writing about the possessions of others.

Exercise 2: The Seasons of Childhood

Many of our childhood memories are associated with seasons or holidays. For this exercise, I'd like you to pick a specific season (or holiday) from childhood and use the <u>outline</u> below to recreate a scene or setting. Then focus on an event or events that occurred during that time and at that place. Use the <u>lead</u> provided below the outline words to help you research the event through short bursts of Directed Freefall.

Outline

- Year and season (or holiday):
- The place:
- My age and school grade:
- Family members around at the time:
- Family members not around at the time:
- Friends I had then:
- Possessions related to this time and place:
- Event(s) related to this time and place:

Leads

- I have chosen to go back to this time and place because...
- One event I associate with this time and place is. ...
- I am thinking about this event because...
- I see... I hear... I feel... I smell... I taste... I sense...
- The dominant emotion I associate with this event is...
- If I could say one thing to someone there at the time, it would be...

- If I could say one thing to someone not there at the time, it would be…
- If this event were the basis of a story or a poem, it would be titled…

Feel free to complete a five-minute Freefall once you have completed the above exercise….

Exercise 3: In the Home Where I Grew Up

Sit somewhere comfortable and think about a <u>room, just one room,</u> in the home where you grew up. You might think about several rooms at first, but I want you to close your eyes and focus on one room. Once you have picked a room on which to focus, start to recreate the room in your mind.

With your eyes shut, visualize yourself walking around the room. What do you see, hear, smell, feel, taste? Imagine yourself in the room on a specific day or at a particular time in your life. What do you see? Who else do you see? What is going on? What isn't going on?

When you open your eyes, use the <u>leads</u> below to help you write about what you just visualised, then flip into a five-minute Freefall or use the last line of the leads as the first line of a Directed Freefall. Alternatively, feel free to Cluster—using the name of the room as your key word—and then Freefall.

Leads

- The year is_____
- I am _____ years old
- The room is_____
- I have chosen it because…
- I look around and see…
- I also see…
- In addition, I see…
- I (hear/feel/smell/taste)…
- What I am doing there is…
- Now what happens is…
- Thinking back on what transpired in that room, I feel…

Exercise 4: Photographic Journey

Think of a favourite photograph from childhood (you might want to find some old photos to use for this exercise). Using the following leads to guide short Freefall bursts.... (If you can't picture a picture or find a photo, try to freeze a particular moment in your mind.) Then write a Directed Freefall using the line provided or produce your own opening line and Freefall.

Leads

- I have a picture of...
- In the picture, I look...
- Also in the picture are...
- I was the kind of kid who...
- Thinking back, I remember...
- And this memory leads me to...
- The emotion I felt then was...
- The emotion I feel now is...
- If I could have this picture taken over again, I would...

Directed Freefall line:

Every picture tells a story, and this picture from childhood tells a story of....

Exercise 5: Life with Parents

Use the leads provided below to help you express childhood feelings about your parents or guardians. While I have primarily used the word "Father" in the leads, feel free to focus on your mother or father or on your significant guardian. You can also go through the exercise twice—once for the significant male influence in your life and once for the significant female influence.

Leads

- When I think about my father's life before I was born, I see a man who....
- Some of the most important experiences in his early life were....
- When I think of my father at home, I see him....

- He was the kind of father who....
- When I think of the similarities between my parents, I see....
- When I think of their differences between my parents, I see....
- Some similarities between my father and me are....
- A question I have never asked my father is....
- I would like to ask this question because....
- I would like him to answer it by saying....
- He would probably say....
- If my father were to describe me as a child, he would say....

If so inspired after completing these leads, flip into Freefall. Or simply take a well-deserved break.

Journal Exercise

If any of the above writing exercises inspires you to explore childhood events further, use your journal to do so. You can explore events based upon the above exercises, or investigate other events inspired by these exercises or that simply pop into mind. Use the structure of these exercises to help you on your journey. Or Cluster key words and Freefall.

Don't be afraid of the truth as you remember it**, but don't be afraid to push your memory into the creative lies of fiction** or the shape of poetry (more on this in subsequent chapters). In other words, use your memories as beginnings or springboards. Dive off them and see the depths to which your writing can take you.

What do you do with all the writing? That is for you to decide. Some gesture sketches are worth framing. Others are worth exploring further. Some form the basis of the final picture. Others get tossed. As mentioned, distance (time away from your raw creation) will help you decide. And there will be more information on what you might do with your work later in the book. So do not toss any pages or delete any files!

For now, let's continue our Journey Through Childhood in the next chapter.

Chapter 6: Journey through Childhood II

Getting Started

How was your journey though childhood? Some people have accused me of attempting to perform therapy. Nothing could be further from my intent, although there is no denying that the exercises can be cathartic, painful, enjoyable, entertaining, boring, exhilarating... All that is secondary to capturing and recreating emotions, which are at the heart of writing that begs to be read.

Think about how you react to what you read. Which do you prefer: flat, two-dimensional characters or fully developed characters who seem to live and breathe? I think you know my take on this, and infusing your characters—when and where appropriate in a story—with emotions that are real and raw is one way of creating fully-developed characters.

Journal Exercise

I'd like you to tackle one last Journey through Childhood exercise. Before you get to the exercise, start by reading *The Nuncles*, below. *The Nuncles* is based on very real memories that I have of several of my uncles. Yes, the memory is exaggerated and pushed into fiction; however, the memory and underlying emotions are very real.

The Nuncles

They were as tall as hydro poles, and wider around the chest, the Nuncles were. Their arms and legs were as thick as Toronto telephone books, which, like the Nuncles arms and legs, grew thicker each year. Their hands were always clenched in huge iron mallets that could bust concrete slabs into dust, unless they were stooping to pick me up. Then they thrust out beefy drumsticks fingers that scooped me off Grandpa's Ossington Avenue porch and held me high, the Nuncles did. In their hands, I became a vestal virgin they were compelled to thrust high and sacrifice to the Sun.

But before they tossed me salad-like into the sky, they held me close to their crazy man-in-the-moon howling faces, pockmarked with deep, black craters and pits and bursting with red and yellowish volcanic pustules that looked as if they could explode at any moment.

They were the Nuncles, at least that's what I called my American uncles. I was in awe of them; they scared me shitless.

As they lifted me, I would try to grab onto something, anything—even their oceans of hair, slicked back black waves that crashed over their pimply foreheads as they shook their heads. I tried to break their grasp, but to no avail, as the Nuncles exploded with hyena laughter and tossed me like a dwarf, from Nuncle to Nuncle to Nuncle, from drumstick hand to drumstick hand. Gaining greater height with each toss. Then up. Up. Up.

Tossing me from Nuncle to Nuncle to Nuncle, they'd toss me off the porch, then toss me higher than the first floor window ledge, then higher than the top of the window, then higher than the porch roof itself.... Up higher. Higher. Higher.

Higher than the electrical wires that ran from scarred wooden hydro pole to pole down Ossington Avenue—the prickly static electricity of the hydro wires causing my brush cut to stand up on end. Up higher than the second floor windows. Then higher than the third floor windows. Then higher than the peaked roof of Grandpa's pinched, red brick, semi-detached Victorian house. Up higher than the tall maple in the yard. Up past startled birds. Up to the clouds. Up through the clouds. Up until the heat of the sun singed the cropped hairs on my head.

That's how high they claimed to toss me. What did I know about how high they tossed me? I dared not open my eyes once airborne, for fear they spoke the truth. For fear that it was all true. For fear that it was all a lie. For fear of pissing myself.

Although the thought of pissing down upon the heads of the Nuncles is something that I might have fantasized, if I had had the wits and courage to do so then. Instead, I let them toss me as I suffered wave upon wave of nausea. I let them toss me until they bored of the game. Until they shouted with far too much glee: "Enough? Had enough? Say *Uncle* if you've had enough. Say *Uncle*..." And as if on cue, I would stutter-wail: "N-n-n-nuncle. N-n-n-nuncle. N-n-n-nuncle!" Three times I would wail, one for each of the cruel fools—my American uncles....

Now What?

So those were *The Nuncles*. Now what? Now think back to childhood, perhaps between the ages of 6 to 12. Create a list of adults. Adults who frightened you. Adults who made you laugh. Adults who made you run and hide. Adults you ran to and hugged. Adults you were in awe of. Adults who inspired you or somehow moved you. Adults who, for better or for worse, were a part of your life.

Pick one adult or, if appropriate, one group of adults. Give the adult or the group a nickname, something that describes them to you. Even if you did not have a name for them as a child, even if it might not mean anything to a reader, initially, give them a nickname.

Once you have your nickname, use that name as your Cluster key word, and Cluster like crazy. When you are done, when you feel you have captured every physical aspect and emotional sensation, as well as any key incidents/events in your relationship, flip into Freefall....

When you flip into Freefall, try to paint a detailed, fantastical word. Heap it on. Pile it high. Over do it. Then over do it again. And again. No holds barred. Even if your editor screams in furry at you, "Enough. Too much. Too far." Take it further then. Push it higher, wider, deeper...

Who cares what you say as you write your version of *The Nuncles*? This is for you, for your journal. Later, no rush, if you feel you have something, you can always tone it down or pull it back. Or heap more on it. That is the wonder of the writing process. Write now. Put it away. Edit later.

With that in mind, make your list (if you have not done so already). Pick one adult or one group of adults. Assign a nickname. And go...

So, if you are ready, write down your key word—the <u>nickname</u>—and...

<u>**Begin your Cluster....**</u>

(Don't forget to <u>flip into Freefall</u> when you feel the urge to write.)

Now What?

So what do you do with all the Journey Through Childhood work that you have written?

I don't believe in using definitions—defining short stories or poetry for you and then saying, "OK, based on that definition, turn what you have written into a short story or a poem." That is simply inviting the editor to impose form upon your raw research, your rough drafts, you introspection, your creative endeavours—before you or the work are/is ready for form. Besides, this book is all about the joy of writing.

Ah, but publishers, editors, readers require–demand–form, you say.

And I have no problem with form. In fact, we will look more at form later in the book. Right now, my hope is that your gestures are beginning to take shape almost organically—that you are starting to find your voice and create in a more confident manner. And that you are having fun!

There will be ample time for revision and for imposing form. Having said that, if you have a sense of what you would like to try to do with some of your sketches, feel free. At the same time, if you want to carry on with writing exercises, please do so. There is no rush to grow up, be an adult and impose form on your work. But to help you slowly evolve in that direction, we will use, in the next chapter, a writing exercise called *Modelling* to help you shape work—still without invoking the editor. We want to work within form in a way that keeps the emotional heart of your work (of your creation) beating.

Before you move on, take a moment and go back over the work you have created based on the Journey through Childhood exercises and review several Freefalls. How interested are you in what you have written? Can you see expanding on your work? If it you fee like it, pick one piece of work that intrigues you and conduct the Delta factor exercise with it. See where it goes.

Or simply read on and continue to write....

Chapter 7: Cheese Sandwiches and Motivation

Cheese Sandwiches

This seems like as good a time as any to take a break for lunch... I mean to pause and reflect. *To reflect on what?* you ask. How about *cheese sandwiches*?

Now I happen to like cheese sandwiches—a Kraft processed cheese single slice on white Wonder Bread smothered with margarine. But that's probably because such sandwiches evoke rather powerful memories from childhood. My logical side, the side of me that enjoys spicy Thai food for instance, cannot think of anything blander than a Kraft processed cheese single slice on white Wonder Bread smothered with margarine. Maybe you can. If that's the case, you reflect on that while I reflect on cheese sandwiches.

Why Cheese Sandwiches?

The Canadian author, Alistair McLeod (*No Great Mischief*) suggests writers should fear cheese sandwiches. Why? Imagine your reader putting down your just published novel or collection of short stories or poetry to head off to the kitchen to make... a cheese sandwich... and never returning to your book. Imagine if the allure of a bland, boring, tasteless, dull, dry cheese sandwich is more compelling than the allure of... your writing!

Ouch.

However, before you let that fear—the fear that a reader will replace your work with a cheese sandwich—grab you by the neck and throttle the writing life out of you, ask yourself this: What motivates the reader?

I'd suggest it is *Hunger*. A hunger to be entertained or informed. Or informed in an entertaining manner. Or entertained in an informative manner. Nothing more. Nothing less. You, as writer, have no control over what motivates the reader. And you have no control over how readers will react to your writing. The reader has the right to react in any way he or she chooses based on the full range of his/her life/emotional experiences. *You have no control over that.* So don't try to control it. Control your writing. That is your job! (Even if this book seems to imply that you have to *lose control* of your writing first.)

Think of the books you loved that others loathed, or the movies you loathed that

(re)Discover the Joy of Creative Writing

others loved. When it comes to literature, or any form of entertainment, we are entering an incredibly subjective realm. In other words, develop a thick skin and expect to lose some readers to cheese sandwiches, You have no control over that. But work to make your writing as entertaining and/or informative as you can. In short, work hard at your craft. Be true to your vision. Listen to constructive feedback. Accept what makes sense; ignore the rest. The reader will do what the reader will do regardless of what you do.

And if you haven't tried a Kraft processed cheese single slice on white Wonder Bread smothered with margarine in a while, give it a shot. It's not as bland as it sounds. (However, if you want to really jazz it up, add a crisp leaf of iceberg lettuce to it. *Yum!*)

What Motivates You?

So if you do not have control over what motivates the reader, or how the reader will react to your writing, what do you have control over? Your work. And, I would suggest, your own motivation. While I hope readers stick with my work, I would not be offended if a reader left my work behind for a cheese sandwich. *I would think twice about my motivation if I left writing behind for one.* Having said that, I do stop for lunch, and sometimes lunch is rather bland—but I do not drop my writing to have bland meals. I stop writing when I am famished and need some food, any food, to refuel me so I can carry on. There is a difference!

What motivates you? Why do you want to write? You are about half way through the book. Maybe it's a good time to think about it or even Freefall on it.

Directed Freefall, Anyone?

If you want to try a Directed Freefall, here is a line to get you going:
- *"I write because..."*

Or Cluster the word *Motivation* and see what you come up with. Then flip into Freefall.

Or Cluster the phrase *cheese sandwich*. Then flip into Freefall.

Or simply start writing..... Go. Write....

Seriously. Go. Write.

Come back in 10 or 15 minutes, or an hour or so, and read the rest of this Chapter. Go. Scoot. Write!

Welcome Back!

What motivates me? If you were to ask me that question, I'd have difficulty answering it. For me, writing is like a drug. Perhaps it is a drug. I am writing this on New Year's Day. I could be doing many things, but I am writing.

I heard Alistair McLeod talking about cheese sandwiches and it kind of exploded in my head (his talk did...not a cheese sandwich). The talk got me thinking about the reader and the writer, and what motivates each of us. I can't clear the debris from my cranium until I put it down on paper.

I *have* to write this or it will keep me up at night, as it did last night—3:00 a.m. as I was mulling over cheese sandwiches. I'll be darned if I'm going to mull it over tonight, so I am purging my thoughts. Making them whole by writing them down. Somehow, the need to do so is what motivates me.

Am I informing you? Entertaining you? That is not my responsibility. I have no control over how you react to my writing, this chapter or the book. I simply know that I have something to say and I must say it. I don't *need* an audience to *need* to write. *I have the need to write, and that is all I need.* If this informs you and/or entertains you in some way... Bonus.

I would write this without you as part of the equation. You are here. You are part of the equation, but you are not what motivates me. This pressure inside, building... Hot magma about to spew... That's what causes me to erupt upon the page.

It's not always there. But when it is, I ignore it at my sleep-deprived peril.

Like many freelance writers, I have been able to harness this pressure, this potential energy. I harness it when I write the non-fiction work for which I am paid. But it harnesses and directs me when I write about writing and when I create short stories, personal essays and poetry.

So... Have I motivated you to go for a cheese sandwich yet? Or are you still with me? Have you written about what motivates you? If not... Go. Now. Do it.

Motivation and *What If?*

Guess what? What motivates you is immaterial. (*Oh, now he tells me!*) By that, I mean what motivates you to write is no doubt different from what motivates me to write, and who cares? From the perspective of the story or the reader, what does it matter why you write?

Oh, maybe one day, if you become a famous writer, journalists will ask what motivated you, but that will not change one word of what you have written.

So why this exercise? First off, I hope you found it a fun and perhaps somewhat thought-provoking writing exercise. Beyond that, it helps to be conscious of what motivates you to write so you can harness that energy—especially if you are feeling down or otherwise preoccupied. Figure out what motivates you to write and you will most likely write more often so you can reap whatever reward you reap when you write.

Having said that, when you are writing all you have to be concerned about is this: *What motivates the story*. What motivates the story may be, most likely will be, different with each story (or poem) you write. What motivates the story is different from what motivates you (even if some of your motivation seeps into the story). And if what motivates your story to move forward—plot and character development, for instance—resonates with what motivates the reader to read, bonus!

At the same time, there may be times when you want to deliberately set out to motivate readers to read your work. That works most often if you write specific genres such as romance, murder mystery, science fiction and so on. Readers of specific genres tend to be motivated by the structure of writing—the way the plot unfolds, twists and turns and the way the characters interact and develop.

Of course if you want to write a specific genre you have to spend time reading books written in that genre. You have to analyse how they are structured and what makes them work, then you have to recreate that with your own cast of characters and plot. However, the exercises you are engaged in here can help you no matter what you want to write—private journal entries, short anecdotes, short stories, literary novels or genre-specific novels, and even poetry. Continue to Freefall and Cluster in your Journal on a regular basis. The journal exercises you do will help you find ideas you might want to tackle and they will also make you a better—a more invigorated and motivated—writer.

Speaking of motivation, yet again, you might say a story without motivation is like a day without sunshine—as dull as that cliché is. And a dull story, no matter what your personal motivation for writing, will motivate the reader to head for... a cheese sandwich.

What if? Sparks the Story

I want to separate what motivates you to write and what motivates the story to move forward—separate what sparks or inspires you to write a particular story from what sparks the plot and other elements of the story.

In an upcoming chapter, you can read a short story, *The Conquest Of Kong*. What you don't see in that story is the inspiration behind it.

You don't see the author, a middle-aged man, occasionally reflecting on how he and his father never really connected. You don't see how that feeling of disconnectedness returns one day like a storm when the man is on the midway of the Canadian National Exhibition (CNE). You don't see why it returns: you don't see how the trip to the CNE rekindles the childhood memory of the author and his father at a small fair where the father was enticed by the lure of a Carney into playing a game that was almost impossible to win. You don't see the father winning several times. You don't see the Carney calling him back to the game after each win, until the father, going after the big prize, child at his side, loses.

What inspired the story was one thought that hit like a blinding flash as the author stood on the midway, surrounded, almost overwhelmed, by the sights and sounds and smells of the CNE:

What if I could have helped him win?

That was it. *What if?* That's what inspired the story—*What if?*—and inspires many stories.

It is *What if?* that lets the author create characters and plunk them down in time and space, and have them interact and relate with each other and secondary characters until the question is answered. But in creating this story, the author (Paul Lima) no longer exists. The "I" of the story is a character of my creation, but he is not me. He assumes a life and a quest of his own. And it his quest that motivates, or moves forward, the story. In other words, my father/son psychobabble no longer matters. My lust for the drug of writing is immaterial. And whatever readers may or may not think of what I create is out of my control.

However, without that *What if?* inspiration, I would not have had a story. If the question had not hit me, there would be no work of fiction. Without *What if?* I would not have pushed the truth, as I remember it, into the wonderful lies (or perhaps larger truths) of fiction.

As you write—especially as you do the exercises in this book and write in your journal—you don't have to be aware of *What If* questions. However, sometimes the act of writing without that awareness can lead you to a *What if* question that might inspire a story. At the same time, something you see, hear, do, read, smell or touch might be inspired to write. You might find a story inside you that feels like magma about to explode. When that happens, find your journal—you might want to carry a journal and pen or portable computing device with you—and write. <u>Go. Create. Write like a dervish. Get down whatever comes up.</u>

Later, in a more rational moment, after you have completed your humble first draft, you can read it over and ask yourself: *Now what do I want to do with this?* The answer might be *nothing* or it might be *something*. I think you can tell by now that what is more important, as far as I am concerned, is that you left yourself open to inspiration and you wrote.

Journal Exercise

If you are at all inspired by the concept of *What if*, take a moment and review some of the writing you have done. See if you can find a *What if* question underlining any of your writing. If you find it, write it out in full: *What if...?* (whatever the question seems to be). Use that question as the opening line in a Directed Freefall and see where your writing takes you.

Try to do this with at least three passages or see if you can come up with at least three *What if* questions that inspire you to Freefall.

What If? Discovery

After writing the first draft of this chapter, I came across a passage on *What if?* by the novelist John Irving (*The World According to Garp, Cider House Rules, Hotel New Hampshire, The Fourth Hand* and others). It seems most appropriate, so I've inserted here.

John Irving writes:

Janet [his wife] gave me the idea for The Fourth Hand. One night we were watching the news on television before we went to bed. A story about the nation's first hand transplant got our attention. There were only brief views of the surgical procedure, and hardly a word about how the patient—the recipient, as I thought of him—lost his hand in the first place. There was nothing about the donor. The new hand had to have come from someone who'd died recently; probably he'd had a family.

Janet asked the inspiring question: "What if the donor's widow demands visitation rights with the hand?"

Dr. John C. Baldwin, the Dean of Dartmouth Medical School, has assured me that this probably wouldn't happen in what we call real life—not without the unlikely concurrence of enough lawyers and medical ethicists to start a small liberal-arts college. But I always listen to the storytelling possibilities. Every novel I've written has begun with a "What if..."

Just as the memory of an incident from childhood can spur the imagination and inspire a story, so can almost any interesting *What if* question. In addition, the answers to such questions (in other words, the stories such questions inspire) can keep your reader reading by keeping them engaged by the quest to answer the question. If your story pursues the answer to *What if?* and does so in a manner that engages the reader, you will keep the reader from reaching for that cheese sandwich that all writers (whether they know it or not) fear.

Does It Always Have to be *Me*?

In the *Conquest of Kong* example, the inspiration for the story comes from within me—from within my realm of memory and experience. But as Irving indicates, inspiration can come from outside one's memories. For instance, issues with my father aside, I could have seen a father try in vain to win a prize for his son on the midway and could have been inspired to write a story about it: *What if the son could help or inspire his father to win?* By asking *What if?*, I suddenly have two characters engaged in a quest or the beginning of a story.

What you see, read and hear generally has to somehow resonate with your life experiences to inspire you. But not always. It depends on how curious you are. And the extent to which you are able to internalize sensations beyond your realm of experience and create fiction based on what you observe.

If you are finding the concept difficult to grasp, or even if you are grasping it, but you want to see it in action, here is a little game you can play. Read something—a short story or novel—or think of a work of fiction you have read, then work backwards and see if can find or summarize the *What if* inspiration.

Recently, I read John Irving's *A Widow for One Year*. I don't know what his *What if?* question was, but here is my attempt at a *What If* summary:

> *What if a teenage boy falls madly in love with, and has a relationship with, an older woman—and then does not see her again for 25 years?*

This *What if* inspires an amazing journey, with an amazing cast of characters in *A Widow for One Year*.

Can Your *What If* Change?

Once you find inspiration, are you stuck with the triggering *What if?* Not at all.

I know the *What if* question that inspired *Last Summer at Barebones* (a novel I referred to earlier in the book) changed as the novelist worked on the book. In fact, the book started out as a short story inspired by: *What if a young girl is expecting to have the best summer of her life and it turns into the worst summer of her life?*

As Diane Baker Mason, the novelist, explored that concept in a short story, she found herself asking: *What if a young girl is expecting to have the best summer of her life and it turns into the worst summer of her life, and the young girl blamed her older sister? Why?* As she answered the first question, she discovered/created a powerful antagonist with whom the young girl locked horns.

Many words into what was becoming a novel, the *What if* question shifted, or expanded, yet again: *What if a young girl expecting to have the best summer of her life has the worst summer of her life and blames her older sister, and the negative impact of that summer is so strong that ultimately the younger sister vows the most extreme revenge–murder?*

If you were to read the opening of the novel, you might think that the *What if* question above was the first question asked. It wasn't. However, since that is what inspired the final story, it should come as no surprise that it shaped the novel. But if you read the novel analytically, you will see the evolution of the *What If* questions. But we are now into the academic claptrap that often spoils the read! So enough of that.

So Now What?

If you have not already done so, look at some of what you have written. Try to find the inspiration for your writing, or see if what you have written can be used to inspire a *What if* statement. If you don't see the *What if*, dig beneath the surface to find it. Ask yourself:

- What is my main character(s) trying to accomplish? Why?
- What/who stands in his/her way? Why?
- Will he overcome the obstacle(s)?
- If so, how and why? If not, why not?

The answers to these questions will help you plot and shape your story, if you want to do more with something that you have written.

Important: Do not let this quest for inspiration interfere with the creative process. Seldom does it all come together in one shot. My first drafts of *The Conquest of Kong* were miserable even though I was inspired and the story felt motivated. I had something I wanted/needed to say but was not saying it. It took me a while to understand the implications of the inspiration, before I could more clearly tell the story. But I did not let this lack of focus prevent me from creating. Without the initial work, I would have never discovered (and finished) the story I wanted to tell.

Journal Exercise

Try to create *What if* scenarios of your own and see what kind of writing that inspires. Pose the *What if* question and flip into Freefall. It's that simple. But if you need some help, here are a few simple *What if* exercises to get you started:

Pick any of these *What if* scenarios and use them as opening lines of Directed Freefalls:

- What if a character found a million dollars in a gym bag at the zoo?
- What if a character could fly? [What if pigs could fly?]
- What if global warming destroyed life as we know it and left your main character living in a colony of 12 people?
- What if global warming destroyed life as we know it and left your main character, who was gay, living in a colony of 12 people of the opposite sex?
- What if Sally and Diane attended a weeklong writers' conference and, to save money, shared a room with Peter, a writer with whom they were both secretly in love?
- What if you were on a plane that lost power and the captain said, "We have one minute before we hit that mountain up ahead…"? What would you write in the last minute of your life? (Use a timer and write for one minute only.)
- What if Stewart, a brilliant pianist (or artist or hockey player or something *other*) lost his left leg?
- What if Jillian was turned down for a promotion to VP of Marketing and discovered it was because of her gender?
- What if your spouse divorced you and moved to the Cayman Islands and only after your spouse moved, you discovered he or she had won $5 million in the lottery?
- What if you found a fly in your soup at an upscale restaurant?
- *What if you came up with your own What if? and wrote something of interest to you?*

Chapter 8: Modelling to Write

Modelling Overview

Westside Story. Love Story. Both works are modelled on Shakespeare's *Romeo and Juliet*, which was modelled on an older Italian play. In this chapter, you will make like Shakespeare and *model* your writing on works by other writers. The goal is not to simply copy the works of others but to find inspiration through modelling. Why? Let's see what novelist Margaret Atwood has to say...

Word for Thought

"*Read*," is what Margaret Atwood says when asked if she has any advice for neophyte writers.

But why read?

I suggest Atwood means that you should read analytically—that you can learn how to write by analyzing how other writers have created their works and by analyzing the impact that other works have on you.

For instance, I tossed the book, *The Spy Who Came in from the Cold* (by John Le Carré) against the wall in anger when I got to the end. I was not angry at Le Carré; I was angry that a character I had come to know and feel for had died when I wanted him to live. It would make sense that, as I writer, I would get over my hissy-fit and re-read the book to analyze how Le Carré made me care about his fictional creation and how he got such an emotional reaction out of me.

By the way, I would not expect you to react the same way to the novel: as readers, we reserve the right to react any way we please, or any way our emotions or hormones cause us to react. I cried at the end of the first chapter of *Shoeless Joe* by W. P. Kinsella. I knew I was in for a rough ride, but one that I was willing to go on. There is no guarantee that you would feel a thing. What was important, after my emotional reaction, is that I took a deep breath and read analytically—to learn from Kinsella.

If reading can help you become a better writer, then reading analytically can help even more. The next logical step then is to accelerate your learning by <u>modelling</u> other work.

Modelling Confusion

When it comes to modelling, people sometimes confuse this *getting started* writing technique with *plagiarism*. If you copy all or some of another person's work and claim it as your own, you are plagiarising. If you use portions of another person's work in an essay or article without attributing the passage to the author, you are plagiarising.

However, if you find inspiration in the shape, form, subject matter, theme or other elements of another writer's work, you are modelling your work on what you have read. When you model, you find inspiration in the work you are reading, and then you push it further—in any direction that makes sense to you based on your reaction to the work.

I am not suggesting that you model the work of another writer and then rush out to find a publisher for your *new* creation. Modelling is simply an excellent way to inspire and sharpen your creative, analytical, writing and editing skills.

Having said that, let me point out again that Shakespeare's *Romeo and Juliet* was modelled on an older Italian play and that that *Westside Story* and *Love Story* (and more recently *Romeo Must Die*) were modelled on *Romeo and Juliet*. There is no denying the influence of the older works on the subsequent works, so on occasion developing a new twist on an old story works too. Many movies and TV shows are *derivatives* or spin-offs—derived from, spun off of or modelled on characters, plots and/or themes of other movies and TV shows. In most cases, this kind of modelling is done with credit given to the original work that inspired the derivative work. (But not always. Hey, that's showbiz!)

With all that in mind, the goal here is to help you find inspiration, develop characters and create events that ring true with you as writer (so they will ring true with readers). The emphasis is still on creation, but modelling helps impose some sense of form or structure on your work. It should help your creative side work with your editor.

In the exercises below, my instructions are not dictates! Do whatever you feel comfortable with, but try to work on modelling the work presented, at least in your first pass. Now on with Modelling...

Five Modelling Exercises

Modelling can include imitating the form or shape of a poem, the plot of a story, the theme or writing style or another piece of writing, copying the first line and letting it take you wherever (Directed Freefall), or simply finding inspiration in the work. In each of the exercises below, you will be given something to read followed by writing exercises that will help you model the original work in some way.

Exercise One

Short excerpt from *The Girl who Lived in a Shell*:

> *Once upon a time, there was a little girl growing up in middle-class Toronto. She wore black patent leather shoes to church on Sunday, and watched her father sing in the choir. No one in her family argued on Sundays, they just "discussed" the sermon over roast beef and mashed potatoes. There was no alcohol in the house; they all drank ice water with meals....* – author unknown

Modelling Instructions

What goes on at the dinner table can have a great impact on our lives, especially during meals that are served on religious holidays or festive occasions, or when company comes over.

The exercise here is meant to help you create a scene around dinner. You will use Clustering, Freefall and Modelling to help you create your scene. You will take two passes at it—one using a line from the passage above and one using your own opening line so you can move away from the model and find your own voice and emotional centre, allowing you to create a scene that is yours.

Here is what I want you to do:

- Cluster the word **Dinner**
    - Once your Cluster is complete, flip into a Directed Freefall, starting with "Once upon a time...."
- Once your Freefall is finished, reread it. Look for a line in your Freefall to use as the beginning of a new prose piece.
    - Write down that line and try a new Directed Freefall—see where it takes you.

Exercise Two

Excerpt from *President Cleveland Where Are You?* by Robert Cormier:

> That was the autumn of the cowboy cards—Buck Jones and Tom Tyler and Hoot Gibson and especially Ken Maynard. The cards were available in those five-cent packages of gum: pink sticks, three together, covered with a sweet white powder. You couldn't blow bubbles with that particular gum, but it

couldn't have mattered less. The cowboy cards were important—the pictures of those rock-faced men with eyes of blue steel.

On those wind-swept, leaf-tumbling afternoons we gathered after school on the sidewalk in front of Lemur's Drugstore, across from St. Jude's Parochial School, and we swapped and bargained and matched for the cards.

Because a Ken Maynard serial was playing at the Globe every Saturday afternoon, he was the most popular cowboy of all, one of his cards was worth at least ten of any other kind. Rollie Tremaine had a treasure of thirty or so, and he guarded them jealously. He'd match you for the other cards, but he risked his Ken Maynards only when the other kids threatened to leave him out of the competition altogether...

Modelling Instructions

This excerpt evokes many 'things'. I am being vague here because I want you to make a list of the 'things' it evokes for you—your personal equivalents. For instance, I'd substitute 'winter' for 'autumn' and 'hockey cards' for 'baseball cards'; you might substitute 'summer' and 'sea shells'.... *Whatever.*

- Pick your season(s) and your thing(s) and jot them down.
- Once your list is complete, reread the passage.
- Go back to an equivalent time and place in your life and Freefall.
    - If it helps get you started, model the opening line—"That was the autumn of the cowboy cards..." Only substitute your season and thing, and Freefall.... See where it takes you.
    - There is nothing you have to do with the Freefall. Or is there? Don't dwell on that now. Simply do the exercise....

Exercise Three

Read the poem by Al Purdy below, and then follow the modelling instructions.

> She wears glasses
> and has a slightly
> intellectual look
> as if she were about
> to read a book,

(re)Discover the Joy of Creative Writing

and then decided
against it

Modelling instructions

After reading the poem, think of somebody you know and focus on one aspect of that person. The aspect could be an article of clothing, hat, gesture, walk, hairstyle, mannerism, way of speaking, etc.

Once you've focused on the person and the particular aspect, write down all the things it might represent (just as glasses are often used to represent intellectualism).

Then write down the *opposites* of what it might represent.

Now try to model the seven-line poem above. Use it as a template to help you shape your poem. Try this for several people.

If you are feeling inspired, write a longer poem about one person. Play with it. Play with form, style, rhyme or lack thereof. Play with expectations, and dashed expectations.... See where it all takes you.

Or...

Model the first line (based on the gender of the person you are thinking of, and the 'aspect' of the person), and Freefall.... There is no wrong way to do this, as long as you write! Again, see where it takes you.

Exercise Four

Read the poem below, by Tamar S. (a Toronto high school student) then follow the modelling instructions.

> I was with my dad
> When I was two
> He was painting
> I think I was two
> He left the room
> For a minute
> BIG MISTAKE
> When he came back
> He almost fainted
> The room was painted purple and red
> And I had a multi-coloured head

But he was proud of me
He still calls me an artist

Modelling Instructions

- Pick a parent (or guardian or other relative). Jot down his or her relationship to you and name.
- Pick a time (you at a particular age) when that person was around.
- Pick an event—something that happened during the time you have picked.
- Pick a consequence—spell it out.
- Pick a name that your parent (guardian or relative) calls you or would have called you if the event had inspired a nickname.
- Now... Model the poem as exactly as you can. Use the same number of lines and line length.... Notice the judicious use of rhyme (fainted, painted; red, head) and the effect it has. Try to model the rhyme as well and the use of CAPITALS.

This might feel like tough work—work that puts your editor and creator in conflict. Your creator might want to ride the wind, meanwhile your editor is saying: "Hold on. This line is too long. The rhyme goes here, not there." That's okay. Let them fight. Or work together. See what you come up with....

Part of what you need to learn is how and when to work with your editor. So go at it. Try it before you read on.

And then...

Once you have slavishly adhered to the form and completed your poem, try a second version. Go through the same "pick" process you did above, only find someone new. Or use your above "picks."

Then use the opening line of the poem—"I was with my... [whomever] when I was [whatever age]"—to start a Directed Freefall. Run with it: Freefall a long prose passage and see what you create.

And then...

Use the nickname as a keyword, and Cluster it. Flip into Freefall when you have completed your Clustering.

Many options, I know. You can do it all in one sitting, or over several sittings. Either way, the goal here is to write! To find some inner emotion that ends up inspiring your writing.

Exercise Five

Read the William Carlos Williams poem below and then follow the instructions.

This Is Just To Say
I have eaten
the plums
that were in
the icebox
and which
you were probably
saving
for breakfast
Forgive me
they were delicious
so sweet
and so cold

Modelling Instructions

Think of something you've done that a nagging voice in the back of your mind occasionally (or frequently) reminds you of and tells you to apologize for. Ideally, this is something you have not apologized for. Mind you, if you are Canadian, you have apologized for everything you have done. I once bumped into a telephone pole and said, "Sorry." But I digress....

Once you've focused on the event and the people involved, Freefall a letter. To help you, divide your Freefall letter into three distinct sections:

- Describe what you did
- Describe why you did it
- Apologise for doing it

If it helps, start your Freefall with "Dear (name)"—the name of the person you are apologizing to.

Once you have written the three-part Freefall letter, read on.

Now...

A letter has one Point of View (POV)—from that of the writer. With that in mind, what I want you to do now is....

- Flip your Freefall around. Answer the Freefall letter with another Freefall letter written in the voice of the person you have apologized to....

That's it. Take the other person's POV and reply. If you want a Directed Freefall line, try this:

I have read what you have to say and....

After your second Freefall, you may want your first Character to reply. And then have your second character reply again.... Your call. Have fun and, as always, see where it takes you.

Flipping POV

Why did I have you flip POV? You may already have some sense... Short stories, novels—even non-fiction articles—look at relationships, incidents, subject matter, and so on from multiple points of view. You need to be able to see whatever it is you are writing from the perspective of more than one character. Yes, you will have a main POV. You might even create a character who is blind to the points of view of all other characters in the story. But there will be others and they will have to interact with your main character. So you will need to write from more than one POV, even if your main character cannot see beyond the end of his or her nose.

With that in mind, go back over the work you have created in the modelling chapter, or in any other chapter, and see if you can introduce other points of view into anything.

If you have a Freefall that has an exceptionally focused POV, write it from the perspective of another character. Play with POV. Have a character who is speaking in one Freefall interact with a character in another. Why not?

Look at your journey through childhood exercises. Are they all written from the POV of you as a child (or from the fictional children you created)? Absolutely fine if they are. However, now is your opportunity to rewrite them from the POV of a sibling, parent or guardian, other adult or other child. Or perhaps you can rewrite a passage keeping your POV but introducing the POV of another character who gets to interact with your first character.

Seeing the same situation or events from multiple points of view will make you a more mature writer and it will help you expand what may seem like short passages into longer, more complex writing.

Other Modelling Exercises

- Pick other poems, short stories or opening paragraphs of novels to model.
- You might want to model a letter to the editor, an editorial, newspaper column or article, a Hallmark card... whatever!

See where modelling takes you. Read. Read analytically. Learn from what you like, and from what does not appeal to you. Apply what you learn. It will make you a better writer.

Chapter 9: The Conquest of Kong

The Conquest of Kong (below) was a Judges' Choice in the *Toronto Star* Short Story contest. It has been published in several literary magazines and in several online electronic 'zines (e-zines). I present it here because I think it exemplifies much of what this book is about.

I've told you about what inspired the story; however, I'd like to tell you a bit about how the story was written. The first draft was written over most of a day using Freefall. I wrote the Freefall after playing with several Clusters relating to my father and my childhood memories of the CNE; I had already decided to set the story at the CNE rather than at the small fair that I mentioned.

After the initial Freefall, I realized that I had to conduct more research (both internal and external) to get the setting and the relationship between the main characters right. Internal research included more Clustering and a variety of journal entries. External research included reading archive material about the CNE and spending another day there. I spent over $100 on games, rides and food trying to recapture the sights, sounds, tastes, smells that I remembered as a child—that I wanted to incorporate into my story.

I no longer have the first draft, but I know many elements of that long-lost Freefall can still be found in the story. The internal research and Freefall gave my editor a great deal to work with in terms of plot, characters, setting and theme. Speaking of theme, if you are familiar with the previously mentioned *Shoeless Joe* (which was made into a feature film called *Field of Dreams*) you might find the theme familiar. It would be an exaggeration to say that my short story was modelled on *Shoeless Joe*, but it is fair to say that I was influenced by the theme of Kinsella's novel. Reading the novel inspired me to address a father and son theme with my writing.

I have said several times during this book that the author has no control over how the reader will react to his or her work. So I run a risk by presenting a work of my own here. You could say, "Well, if that's where these techniques lead, I want out." However, they can lead *you* many places. That's one of the joys of writing: when you put pen to paper (or fingers to keyboard) you never know where you will end up. There are so many possibilities.

This is where I ended up. I present it for you to read so you can see the techniques presented in this book in action, and so you can see that it is possible to start and complete a work using these techniques, and have the work published. There is no exercise following this story. Simply move on to the next chapter.

The Conquest of Kong

By Paul Lima

It was on the congested grounds of the Canadian National Exhibition that father conquered the world-famous ape. The glassy-eyed creature, wearing a New York Yankee baseball cap, glared down at the midway masses from his perch in the Strike Out tent. I sometimes wonder how we must have appeared from Kong's vantage point—my brawny father with premature flecks of grey dotting slicked-back waves and his scrawny kid with the bristled brush cut. Above the crowd the titanic brute, the most coveted prize at the CNE, seemed unconquerable.

I had never been to the Ex with my father. Although stuffed snakes, poodles, giraffes and bears populated our cramped flat, I had only heard about his midway triumphs from Ted McMaster who owns the garage where father works. Ted told me that my father had once been addicted to midway games.

"Your pa would hear the carny's pitch and, next thing you know, he'd be firing balls an' winning stuffed junk for your ma," Ted said. "The winning wouldn't stop 'til the carny flashed the sign what reads, 'We reserve the right to limit players'."

Ted described father's famous midway pitches. The lethargic knuckleball that sunk into the bushel basket with barely a bounce. The three-fingered lob that delicately threaded the narrow milk-can container mouth. The overpowering fastball that knocked the stuffed Krazy Kat clean off its shelf.

"And he was a magician on the mound at Christie Pits too," Ted added. Besides winning carnival games, my father had pitched hardball for a semi-pro baseball team sponsored by Ted's Texaco. Ted claimed the New York Yankees scouted father in 'fifty-six and offered him a contract. "Instead of pumping gas for me, your father should be pitching for the Yanks."

To an impressionable child with few friends, Ted's mythological tales seemed so real. But the hero he described remained a stranger to me—until the day he came out of his self-imposed exile and tossed three strikes to conquer Kong.

I figured Ted had something to do with the fact that my father was taking me to the

Exhibition because he walked us to the TTC stop, ushered us aboard the Bathurst streetcar and then stood there winking and waving as we headed south. As the packed trolley jerked forward, the change Ted had given me jingled in the plastic coin holder I squeezed in my pocket.

Father and I spent most of our day at the Ex twisting our spines, rattling our brains and flipping our stomachs on daredevil rides. Father even helped me climb the moving steps into the Magic Carpet Ride and he gave me an illicit boost above the red "you-must-be-this-tall-to-ride-the-Flyer" line so I could ride the roller coaster with him.

Between rides, we dodged cow-pies and horse flies in the Coliseum, lived better electrically in the Better Living Building, clambered up and down the winding Shell Tower stairway and watched films of the Leafs capturing their third straight Stanley Cup in the Hockey Hall of Fame.

Down to loose change for the streetcar ride home, we topped off our day with a free-sample feast of pizza and Coke in the Food Building.

"Did you have fun today, Josh?" father asked as I devoured the last of my handouts. I nodded and wiped sauce off my face with the back of my hand. "Then let's get you cleaned up and head for home."

"But we haven't played any games yet," I protested. "I promised Ted I'd win him something."

"If you do everything today, there'll be nothing left for next year," father said as he reached out and knuckled my brush cut.

Hand-in-hand, we wove our way through the rancid mist of concession-stand sizzle that hung over the fair grounds. The early-evening midway was illuminated by sunset hues and neon lights and rocked by unruly rhythms pouring through scratchy speakers. Streams of midway carnies bellowed well-rehearsed come-ons at us.

"Step right up. Step right up!"

"One toss is all it takes."

"Dawwggie dawwggie."

"Knock 'em over. You're a winner."

Father barely glanced at the men who beckoned us with their siren songs—until we rounded the curve in the long sweep of games that brought us face-to-face with King Kong. Father halted so abruptly that I stumbled forward several strides before his arm jerked me back.

"Pa!" I complained.

The mighty ape, his Yankee cap slung sideways, swayed in a light breeze. My father's grip went slack. He gestured upwards. "Lookit, Josh. Gotta have him."

◈ ◈ ◈

Father never did sign the Yankee contract.

"He was scheduled to pitch at Christie Pits the day it was offered," Ted told me. "I was kinda acting like his agent and I suggested he save his John Hancock 'til after the game. 'Show 'em your best stuff then hit 'em up for a few more bucks,' I told him."

Besides the Yankee scouts, my mother, eight months pregnant, was also at the game.

"Your folks was real excited, dreaming big league dreams," Ted continued. "Top of the seventh, your pa working a no-hitter, the lead-off batter smashes a foul ball into the bleachers. It comes straight at your ma. She doesn't duck in time and she gets hit right in the side of the head. I don't know if it was the hit or fall that caused her to go into labour, but you was born in the ambulance on the way to the hospital. Your ma, bless her soul, didn't make it."

And father hadn't thrown a pitch since my birth.

◈ ◈ ◈

King Kong swung from his perch above a splintered plywood cut-out of Yogi Berra, the all-star Yankee catcher. Below the ape stood a pudgy, cigar-smoking carny watching father watching Kong.

"Twenty-five cents a toss," the carny barked. "Twenty-five cents a toss. Be a hero. Be a champ. Wins a monster for your lady. Wins a monster for your love. One ball is all it takes. Twenty-five cents a toss."

The object of the Strike Out game was to pitch a baseball through the hole in Yogi's leather trapper. A scruffy teenager, egged on by laughing cohorts, laid several quarters on the counter. His first pitch missed the catcher completely. The next knocked Yogi's hinged head back. A third bounced off the leather mitt and the hapless adolescent sulked away.

"Who's next now? Who's next?" the carny squawked. The impatient barker yammered at a passing couple. "Are you up to it, sonny? Wins a monster for your lady." When the man refused to nibble, the barker sang, "Is he up to it, ma'am? Is yer man up to it at all?" The girl blushed and looked away.

The beefy barker called out to father. "Life ain't no spectator sport, mister. Twenty-five cents buys you a toss."

I tugged my father's hand. "I've never seen you pitch before, Pa."

My father took a sharp breath. "One toss," he agreed and placed a quarter on the counter.

The carny snapped up the two bits and bared several yellow teeth. "Has we gots ourselves a winner? Has the mighty Kong met his match?" His bellows drew more spectators towards the tent. The carny inhaled on his cigar and tossed father a ball. "Throws one strike," he mumbled, "an' ya wins yerself a small prize."

"You said I win Kong."

"I says ya wins a monster." From under the counter he pulled a small, stuffed monkey. "An' this is a monster. Throws another strike, an' ya can trades up to a bigger prize. Does it a third time in a row an' Kong's yers."

Father massaged the stitches on the baseball then nodded his assent. The carny flashed his yellow grin. "It's man against beast. We're tossing for keeps."

I looked up at the monstrous Kong and shivered.

Father hunched his shoulders several times. He flexed his left arm, hitched his jeans, kicked a small stone out from under his foot, then went into his wind-up. Thwump. The baseball squeezed through the hole in Yogi's glove and struck the back of the tent. A buzz surged through the crowd.

It's true, I thought. You are a magician on the mound.

"Well-a-well-a-well," sang the surprised barker. "We gots a one-toss winner. Does the man plays on an' risk this beautiful creature?" He handed me a musty-smelling monkey. Father looked at him quizzically. "Didn't I tells ya? If ya misses I gets my monster back."

Father shrugged his shoulders and exchanged a quarter for a new ball. As he stared at Yogi's glove, I imagined him on the mound at Yankee stadium—shaking off signals and scowling at batters. He went into his wind-up. Thwump. A clean strike. People whistled, hooted and applauded. The carny shoved another monkey at me. Stuffing spilled from a hole in its neck. Father fished for a third quarter.

"Tells ya what," the carny muttered. "Takes yer prizes and disappears. Comes back later an' I'll gives ya a fiver."

"I'll take my last ball." father flipped the quarter in the air.

"Well-a-well-a-well," sang the carny as he snared the coin. "We're going all the way today." He rolled a baseball in his hands. "Your pa's good," he said to me. "Best I seen in thirty years."

"He coulda pitched for the Yankees."

The carny gummed his cigar. "But he's not a Yank, is he Josh'a?" With a flick of his wrist, father snatched the ball from his pug-faced antagonist. The carny's smirk vanished

(re)Discover the Joy of Creative Writing

in a cloud of grey smoke. ""Well-a-well-a-well. It ain't over 'til it's over."

My father heaved the baseball at the plywood Yankee. The wild pitch snapped Yogi's hinged head back. The crowd groaned. "Bean ball. You lose." The carny whisked the stuffed animals from my arms. "Tough break, kid." He cleared his throat. "Who's next now? Who's next? Twenty-five cents."

My father slapped a quarter on the counter. "Ball," he demanded.

"Save yer two bits, mister," the carny said.

"Let's go, Pa."

"Listens to yer kid."

"My money no good?" father asked, ignoring me as I tugged on his arm.

The carny surveyed the grumbling crowd. "Whadja say, folks? Whadja say? Anyone else keen to play?" Nobody moved. He waved his cigar in father's face. "Well-a-well-a-well. Yer back in the game."

Father cracked his knuckles. Wind-up. Pitch. Thwump. "Keep your monkey," he said as he shoved another quarter across the counter.

"Needs three in a row," the carny reminded us.

Concentrating on the target, father went into his wind-up. Thwump. Yogi's glove barely quivered. Father scrounged his pockets for another quarter. They were empty.

"Hey-hey-hey. Gots to has money to play. Takes a little monster," the carny offered.

My father spun away from the Strike Out counter.

"Wait Pa." With sweaty palms, I squeezed open my change-holder and emptied the money Ted had given me—a dime, two nickels and five pennies—into father's left hand. "Just one toss, Pa."

Rattling the coins as if they were dice, father faced the carny again. "Ball," he whispered and rolled the change across the counter.

"Gonna lets yer kid bails ya out?" Kong's keeper said as he crossed his arms.

"Damn right. The family's winning this one together."

"Play ball," a voice in the crowd shouted.

The carny fumbled under the counter for a ball. He handed it to father who pressed dents into the scuffed leather. "Kind of soft, isn't it?"

"Complaints goes to the gener'l man'ger." A fresh puff of smoke drifted towards father's face.

"I got no complaints, mister."

The carny bowed aside. My father held both hands over his heart, the starting position of his wind-up. He inhaled through flared nostrils, brought his arms over his head… and unleashed a perfect pitch. Smack. The soft rawhide globe struck the glove like an angry fist. And there it sat, stuck in the deep pocket of Yogi's trapper.

"No strike," called the carny as he reached to rescue the ball.

"Don't touch it!" My voice exploded and froze the pudgy man mid-step.

"In! In! In!" chanted the crowd. And through the hole the ball dropped. A tumultuous cheer greeted the victory. People slapped father on the back and raised his arms. Somebody lifted me on to the Strike Out counter as the teen who had lost earlier cut Kong free from his perch. The fallen beast was laid at my feet. His lifeless sockets gazed up at me. A hand liberated the Yankee cap and plunked it on my head. It fell low over my eyes.

Doffing the cap, I took a generous bow. In the centre of acclaim, alone and silent, stood my father. I reached out as he stepped forward and swept me off the counter without glancing down at his conquest.

"Hey," voices shouted. "What about Kong?"

Father tightened his hold on me. Against my chest, I could feel his heart pound. "Don't need no stuffed ape. Don't need him at all." Together, we escaped through the crowd.

"Well-a-well-a-well." The carny revived his song. "Who's next now? Who's next? Be a hero. Be a champ . . . "

As we fled across the fairgrounds, the buzz of mid-way chaos buried his chant. I tugged the Yankee cap back over my eyes, drowning sight, and let father carry me home through the night.

Chapter 10: The Elements of Prose

The Elements of Writing

Do you remember how, earlier on, I said I was not going to give you a bunch of definitions and dry stuff like that? *Well, I lied!* I didn't want the kind of information that I will present here to interfere with the creative process or with keeping creation apart from editing, form and structure when getting started.

This lecture-oriented chapter is meant to help you recognize the elements of prose (we'll look at poetry in another chapter) so you can apply these elements to your work—**after** you have engaged in the creative process. If you are really into Freefall and Clustering, you will find this chapter a complete change of pace. You don't have to do anything with the information here. You can always come back to it when you feel you are ready. On the other hand, if you were looking for structure to help you polish your work, you may find the next few chapters of interest.

Journal Exercise

However, before you start reading the linear lecture, how about another journal exercise?

Put on some classical music, something soothing. Not a march. Or perhaps you might want to use a New Age tape. Use headphones if you have them. Freefall with the music. After 10 minutes, try a change of pace. Rock 'n' Roll. Frank Sinatra. A march. Whatever. If you have one of those CD players with Random Play, put in a mix of CDs and write while your CD player randomly selects music for you, or put your MP3 player or iPod on shuffle and write away.

You may find that the change in music has no effect on your Freefall. At the same time, you may find each change transports you to different places. Kind of like being lost in a malfunctioning "Beam me up, Scotty" machine (Star Trek transporter) and being randomly transported to different worlds.

If you find, after a few attempts, you can't write with a particular kind of music, do not despair. Simply do not use that kind of music. If you like where you go when you play a particular kind of music, stick with it. The whole point here is to get you creating...

So take a bit of time, spin a few tunes, and write along...

The Elements of Writing

This is a very basic chapter. There is so much more that one can say about prose than I say here. You can spend a lifetime studying form, structure and other elements of writing. But will that make you a better writer? Perhaps. As you know from the Modelling chapter, I believe analytical reading can make you a better writer and inspire interesting writing. At the same time, you can study writing to death and not write anything beyond academic essays, if that. Who knows?

What I suggest is that you don't let a lack of *formal* education keep you from writing. And that you don't let an abundance of formal education prevent you from creating. (In other words, don't let the voices of all those pontificating university professors become your internal editor who keeps you from creating.)

It is my contention that many of the elements or prose or poetry end up in your writing naturally, almost organically, when you Freefall or use Clustering and Freefall. But it doesn't hurt to know some of the formal stuff. You can use that knowledge after the fact, as a tool to chisel a story or poem out of that which you have created.

Prose

This *lecture* is written in prose. How can you tell? Well, as my dictionary says, prose "is a literary medium distinguished from poetry especially by its greater irregularity and variety of rhythm and its closer correspondence to the patterns of everyday speech." In other words, you can almost hear me speak this. Also, the words start at the left margin and move to the right without breaking until they reach the right margin. While fiction (sort stories and novels) may on occasion (rare) burst into poetry, fiction is generally written in prose. (By the way, poetry may also, on occasion, burst into prose: a prose poem.)

The Elements of Fiction

What is fiction? Simply put, fiction is "an invented story." However, the most powerful fiction, contain emotional truths to which readers can relate. Whether short story or novel, fiction shares most of the following elements: point of view, setting, character(s), dialogue, mission, action, conflict, plot, climax and denouement. We'll take a quick look at several elements.

Characters

We will look at characters in detail in the next chapter. In short, characters are the people (animals, creatures) that populate your fiction. All stories contain major characters and most contain a supporting cast of minor characters. The major characters include a protagonist or hero, (who tends to dominate the action) and an antagonist or opponent (the one who acts against, opposes or butts heads with the protagonist).

Conflict

Conflict is a clash of actions, ideas, desires, or wills—usually between the protagonist and antagonist. The conflict can involve a person (the protagonist) taking on or clashing with another person, small group, society, nature or the physical environment, an alien, some mysterious external force, fate or destiny or himself or herself (in conflict with some element of her/his nature, perhaps physical, mental, emotional, or moral). The conflict starts the story in motion.

Mission

A story really starts when the protagonist, engaged in a conflict, embarks on a mission. The mission may involve some kind of physical or psychological journey. The characters may not know that they are about to embark on a mission, but they are. Either way, when embarking on a mission, a journey (internal or external and sometimes both) takes place. As one professor of mine once said, "No movement, no story." But don't tell that to Samuel Becket (author of *Waiting for Godot* and many other plays). In his works, the characters end up exactly where they started. Or so it seems.

My short story, *The Conquest of Kong*, starts with the young boy and his father at the CNE. Then there is some back-story to let the reader know more about these characters. The story picks up momentum when the main characters embark on their mission (or journey) to conquer Kong—even though they don't know that that is what they are about to do. The action (that which takes place) on the journey is as much internal—the feelings within—as it is external. My hope is the internal feelings and external action build together through a series of events (plot) towards the climax and dénouement.

The climax is pretty much the end of the journey or the resolution of any conflict. In this case, the resolution of the conflict between the father and the carny leads to, and is symbolic of, the beginning of the resolution of conflict that exists between the father and his son.

As you will notice, if you have had time to read *Kong*, the story ends not with the climax but with the dénouement, a short, almost quiet moment or passage after the climax that allows the reader to reflect on all that has transpired. (Kind of like the cowboy riding off into the sunset, if I may resort to a cliché here.)

And if you think I was thinking of any of that as I wrote the story, then you give me way too much credit! To be fair, it is there almost subliminally in the first couple of drafts. My editor then stepped in to help me bring it into focus (or make me conscious of it) so I could further refine it. In short, I create first; I then edit to make the story more like a story.

Change is Good

By butting heads with the protagonist, the antagonist creates conflict and creates obstacles meant to prevent the protagonist from completing his or her mission. Action occurs as the hero (protagonist) works to overcome the obstacles. As she or he overcomes obstacles, the main character's personality traits, strengths, weaknesses, emotional flaws and virtues are more or less made clear to the reader. The protagonist often changes as the story progresses.

Why change? Think of it this way: a static story (one with no turning points) is a dull story (unless you are Samuel Beckett). A static character (one who does not change) is a dull character. While change does not have to be extreme, there should be some noticeable change for a story to work.

When you finish a first draft of a story, ask yourself:
- What was the emotional (physical/financial/intellectual/etc.) state of the main character at the beginning?
- What is the emotional (physical/financial/intellectual/etc.) state of the main character at the end of the story?

To state it simply, if the protagonist started in a neutral or happy state and ends up sad (or dead) you have *tragedy*. If the protagonist started in a neutral or sad state and ends up happy, you have what is known broadly as *comedy*. If the protagonist does not change, you either have an existential composition, a post-modern work of fiction or a story that has gone nowhere. Nothing wrong with any of that, if that's what you want to accomplish. My point? At some point, you have to make conscious choices based on what you are doing and why. That point can come as you are editing your second draft of your work, but it often comes as you are editing your third or fourth draft—after you have put the story away for a while, to let it ferment, so to speak.

Plotting the Action

While action contributes to change, action in itself is not plot. Plot is the events that unfold to create a beginning, middle and end. *Kong* started out as a Freefall in which I found my main characters, minor characters, most of the action and setting. While I had the semblance of plot in my original Freefall, it wasn't until I edited the Freefall that I formalized my plot outline or plan—the sequence of events that make up the story.

Freefall is a great way to discover and develop plot ideas (as well as characters)—to get what feels like a first draft down on paper so you can move forward. Sometimes, especially if you have been mulling an idea in your head for a while, Freefall can produce a well-structured piece of fiction. Most often, though, you have to return to the work and ask yourself if the events that occur make sense, if the order in which they occur makes sense. If anything is missing. In short, if you have a logical plot.

When I work on a second or third draft, I sometimes create a linear outline of my story—a plot outline that indicates who does what in the story, and the order in which events take place. Then I follow that outline, unless my writing takes me off-plot. I'm not afraid to go off-trail exploring because I know that if the new direction does not pan out, I can always come back to where I was in my outline.

Writing is, as I have said, about making choices. Sometimes the choices or possibilities seem limitless. That can be overwhelming. A plot outline can keep you on track, but it does not have to constrain you.

If I may digress.... If writing a novel, consider creating an outline for each chapter. I consider outlines to be part of the writing process, although they can be produced after initial creation has taken place. Outlines can serve as a guide to the process of completing your work.

Sometimes breaking the novel down (known as *chunking*) into chapters and creating an outline for each chapter makes the writing process less intimidating. *How do you eat an apple? One bite at a time.* That's how you write a novel: One sentence, one paragraph, one page, one chapter at a time.

To wit: if you wrote a page a day (double-spaced) you would write 250 words per day. You would in a year (365 days) write 91,250 words. A novel. What's keeping you from writing 250 words per day?

Setting

Setting is the time and place where action occurs. The setting should enhance, not interfere with, the story and make greater action and dramatic tension possible. The setting in a mountain climbing story would be very important and considerable time would be spent describing it. If a couple have returned to a familiar place in order to rekindle a relationship, the setting may serve as a backdrop to the relationship, or it may become the catalyst that spurs a resolution. In an internal monologue, setting might be much less important to the outcome of the story. Or there could be two settings: where the main character is (an older person lying in bed who cannot move) and where the internal monologue takes the reader (perhaps to places where the character grew up, raised a family, fought in a war…).

A story can span a great deal of time through use of flashbacks. The writer should have a fix on the narrative timeline (the time the story spans as it is being told) and the plot timeline (the time the story's action spans). Kong's narrative time line spans the time it takes the narrator to tell the story of how his father conquered Kong. But the plot timeline goes back to before the birth of the narrator courtesy of flashbacks (as told to the narrator by a minor character).

Please do not concern yourself with timelines while Freefalling. Sometimes they occur naturally. More often than not, managing the shifting times and places of any story is the responsibility of your internal editor, as you revise your work.

If you want to see how timelines intersect, rent the movie *Last Orders* with Michael Caine. There are flashbacks within flashbacks, yet you never get lost in time. Better still, as this is a creative *writing* book, buy the novel *Last Orders*, by Graham Swift. The book has an unusual narrative structure: in each section, characters speak for themselves, recounting past and present actions. There is no omniscient narrator, no stand-in for the author, no one who knows more than any one character. Yet you get to know them all, at every point in time where they intersect with the protagonist—who is already dead! Talk about writing from multiple points of view. (Also, if strong multiple points of view intrigue you, you might be interested in Barbara Kingsolver's *The Poisonwood Bible*.)

Look Who's Talking

Kong is a first person narrative. It's told in first person, from the point of view of the son. While it could have been told in first person from the POV of the Father, it would have been a different story. If a story is told in first person all the events that make up the story must come from the narrator (the person narrating or telling the story, not the person writing it—unless you want to include authorial intrusions like Charles Dickens often did, but I suggest you avoid that if you are just getting started).

The story could have also been told in third person by an omnipotent narrator (not a person in the story; more like an external story-telling voice) but I felt that third person would have inhibited the intimacy that I was trying to achieve between my characters. Achieving this intimacy was not a conscious part of the Freefall, but maintaining it through the use of first person was a conscious act of my internal editor.

A third person narrator can either be <u>omnipotent</u> (all seeing) or <u>limited</u>. Like God, an omnipotent narrator would know everything each character is thinking and can present the story from the perspective of multiple characters. This form is more often used in novels (rather than short stories) with complex plots and large casts of characters like historical works that cover generations. <u>Limited third person</u> can be effectively used in short stories and novels.

In limited third person, the narrator can only directly reveal the thoughts and actions of the protagonist. In other words, the narrator stays out of the heads of all other characters. However, the thoughts/actions of other characters can be revealed through the protagonist if minor characters choose to confide in him/her or if the protagonist sees a minor character doing something. Imagine a mystery novel unfolding:

> Johnson woke up in his worn black leather chair that was tucked in close to his cluttered office desk. He heard a thumping noise, lifted his head off his day planner, and realised the noise was coming from inside his head. He groaned, sat up and straightened his rumpled jacket sleeves. That's when it dawned on him: he was still wearing the suit he had worn to Mallory's Bar last night. It looked much worse for his having slept in it, and he was very hung over. Again.
>
> He could remember little of what had transpired during the previous evening beyond entering Mallory's Bar, meeting a gorgeous blonde—had Mallory introduced them or had she just appeared by his side—and buying her a drink. After that? Things were foggier than a rain forest mist.
>
> She must have slipped something into my drink, he thought. Just as that thought entered his mind, he noticed a blood stain, very red and very dry, on his shirt cuff. Before he could investigate it, a thump roused him. This one came from the office door, not his head. He pulled the arms of his jacket down and covered the stain.
>
> "Yeah?" he called. "Door's open."
>
> In walked the blonde. All six-feet two inches of her statuesque beauty. Johnson gulped.
>
> "Tough night after I left?" she asked, moving close to him.
>
> "Tell me about it."

"I take it you'd like to know."

"I've got the big picture," he said, not wanting to tip his hand. "But there are a few details I'm a bit foggy on."

She laughed. "Foggy is exactly how you look."

"But I can see you clearly enough. So tell me this—if we were at the same place at the same time last night, why do I feel as if I've been run over by a dump truck, and why do you look like you've just stepped off the cover of Vogue?"

As the blonde sat at the edge of his desk and leaned in close, Johnson was concerned she might see the blood on his sleeve. He had to think fast—get her out of his office and get changed, without losing sight of her...

This is <u>limited third person</u>. Readers know what Johnson is thinking and how he feels, but they don't know anything about 'the blonde'—not even her name. Nor will we know anything about her unless Johnson finds out. So while the story is told in the third person, the POV is limited to whatever Johnson knows, sees, hears or otherwise discovers.

In the next chapter, we look more closely at character.

Wind Up

Wow, was that an information dump or what? Does your brain hurt? Or was it all old hat? If there is anything that sort of makes sense but not quite, you might want to find out more. There are books on narrative structure. There are courses you can take. You can search the Web.... Again, what I wanted to do here was give you an overview.

Journal Exercises

By now you should have accumulated a small body of work based on your Freefalls, Clustering, Journeys through Childhood and Modelling.

If you look at your work, you may notice that some of what you have written is in first person and some in third. Try rewriting <u>in third person</u> something you've already written in first person. And try rewriting <u>in first person</u> something you've written in third person.

The goal here, beyond the writing exercise, is for you to see what impact using first and third person can have on the tone and style of your work.

Also, examine some of what you have written with this chapter in mind. How story-like is it? What elements are there? Which are missing? Are any of the missing elements crucial to the work? If so, how might you add them?

Let your internal editor make notes about the work, based on the elements presented above. Turn your notes into point form statements—concerning plot, character, setting, etc. Paste the notes into your work (use Post It Notes and attach them to your work or use Insert Comments and insert them into the margins of your word processing files). Insert them where you think you might demonstrate character, expand plot points, make the setting more vivid and so on. Then hand off these comments to your creative side and write....

Perhaps you can step back from something you've written and create a detailed outline: Who does what to whom? When and why? Use point form to jot down a start-to-finish outline. Use each outline point as the opening line in a Directed Freefall and Freefall from point to point. See where that takes you.

Chapter 11: The Characters of Fiction

One could spend an entire chapter on almost any element of fiction. I've chosen to spend a little more time on characters because without characters you have no story. Plot is an essential element, as is conflict. And every story needs a setting, especially if the antagonist is in conflict with nature. In the book *A Perfect Storm* (made into a movie by the same name) you could argue that the story was all about setting. However, if a storm brews up over the ocean and no characters are there to conflict with it, does anybody give a hoot? Perhaps. But not many anybodys.

Characters are the people (animals, creatures) that populate your fiction. All stories contain major characters (protagonist and antagonist, to start with) and most contain a supporting cast of minor characters. A minor character could be the bus driver who takes a major character from point A to point B. Through dialogue or action that has an impact on a major character, a minor character can serve a particular function.

In the following example, a minor character serves a function without doing much of anything:

> Outside the subway station, I caught the Bay bus heading south, heading towards divorce court. Divorce court. Divorce. Who would have thunk it possible. Not I, not 20 years ago when Lydia and I took our vows. Twenty years ago, wedded bliss. And now I am on my way to divorce court—all due to her.
>
> I was totally wrapped up in my thoughts—my divorce court defence strategies—when I handed the bus driver my transfer. But when the driver said "thank you" her voice jolted me out of my reverie.
>
> Good-gawd, I thought. A woman driver. Figures. Here I am unemployed with a wife about to take me to the cleaners over child support and alimony payments I can ill afford and there is a dame driving this rig. She probably has a husband making a mint as a bank executive and her salary is paying for their time-share vacation condo in Hawaii.
>
> "You're welcome," I muttered and moved to the back of the bus...

Simply by existing, the minor character has served a function: she has started in the main character an internal monologue that helps reveal a great deal about the character's attitude towards women. No doubt, his attitude will come into play as the story progresses.

The major characters, as I've said, include a <u>protagonist</u> or hero, (who tends to dominate the action) and the <u>antagonist</u> or opponent (the one who acts against, opposes or butts heads with the protagonist). Yes, you can have two or more people working together as protagonists, although one usually is seen as *the* main character. And you can have a team of antagonists. Again, one usually dominates.

You do not want stories, particularly short stories, to be overly cluttered with characters. Some fiction, however, has a cast of hundreds. In historical novels that span centuries, heroes and antagonists change from generation to generation (unless there is a vampire or poltergeist that spans generations). Episodic stories might involve a hero interacting with (fighting and defeating) a series of antagonists. For instance, punished by the gods for killing his family (in a fit of insanity inflicted upon him by one of the gods), Hercules has to perform 12 labours—feats so difficult that they seem impossible—each against a different antagonist.

Character Types

There are several types of characters. A <u>flat character</u> is known by one or two character traits. A <u>round character</u> is complex and multi-dimensional. A <u>stock character</u> is a stereotyped character (mad scientist, absent-minded professor). <u>Static characters</u> remain the same from beginning to end. <u>Dynamic characters</u> undergo change. Change must be within the realm of possibility; the character must be motivated and allowed sufficient time to change. Character types used should be appropriate to the genre (romance, mystery, sci-fi, spy, literary) and type (comedy, drama) of story as well as the plot.

Character Differentiation

So that your characters don't all look alike, sound alike and act alike, characters should have distinct features. It is particularly important for you to know your main characters well—to have a solid sense of who they are. Yes, there can be similarities between two major characters, but differences are required. Not all of the character traits will enter into your story, but it doesn't hurt to be aware of the need to differentiate your characters and to create a list of differences on the side. Sometimes you can determine all this before your write, other times these character aspects evolve as you write.

Differences often become apparent as the characters come into conflict, attempt to resolve conflicts and move forward on their journey. These differences help the reader keep the characters separate in their minds. The differences also allow the reader to become engaged with characters as individuals or to feel conflicted over which character(s) to invest emotional energy in. If the reader cannot invest emotional energy in your characters, they will abandon your story.

Have characters started to raise their heads in your writing? Are there characters populating any of your work that you are interested in? Do you have at least two characters in any of your work that you would like to develop? If so, pick two and use the character sketch list below to put flesh on their bones. Get down as much detail as possible. Then go back to whatever you are working on that includes the characters you sketch out here, and start writing again. Or use the journal exercise below to try to further develop your characters.

Character Sketch Exercise

Pick at least two characters you have met through your writing so far, and fill in the blanks in the chart, using as much detail as possible. Get to know your characters as intimately as possible.

Name: Gender: Date of Birth: Born in: city/state: Zodiac sign: Father's Name (and age): Mother's Name (and age): Siblings' Names (and ages): List of important relatives: Serious friends *then* and *now* (names, gender, when they met, first impressions where are they know, if known; dead or alive)… Friends… up to age 5: 5 to 12:	Travel: (where, when & why): Sports: watches / plays: Dreams: yes / no Recurring dream(s): Political Orientation through the ages (see ages in relation to friends): Social causes, if any: Recycler: Yes or No - cans, bottles and plastics, organic matter Hobbies / Interests: Passion(s): Believes in: aliens / God / reincarnation / after life / heaven / hell / the bible Education: (programs, courses, locations of institutions, degrees / diplomas / certificates, etc.) Work Experience: (companies, positions,

(re)Discover the Joy of Creative Writing

12 to 16:
16 to 21:
21 and on...
Height / weight of your main characters at each age above:
Hair colour and style at each age:
Colour of eyes:
Complexion:
Body shape/size:
Bed wetter: (If yes, until age)
Favourite toys:
Major illnesses:
Bones broken:
List of serious and/or memorable accidents:
Pet Peeves:
Favourite Colour:
Least Fav. Colour:
Favourite Food:
Least Fav. Food:
Fav. Dessert:
Fav. Junk Food:
Vegetarian or carnivore
Fav. Movie:
Fav. Song:
Fav. Group/Singer:
Fav. TV shows through the ages:
Fashion sense (describe):
Fav. Clothes

Est moments:
happiest when:
saddest when:
depressed when:

dates from/to)
Current Marital Status:
Previous Marital Statuses:
Sexual Orientation: (hetero, homo, bi-sexual, bi-curious)
First memory (details):
Repressed memories: (details):
First Kiss: (when, with who, how did it happen)
First base: (when, with who, how did it happen)
Second Base: (when, with who, how did it happen)
Third Base: (when, with who, how did it happen)
Virgin or not:
Lost virginity - age, to whom, how:
Most recent sexual experience:
Fav. sexual experience:
Worst sexual experience:
Orgasm: yes / no (self-induced only, with lover(s), when, during...)
Manner in which he/she talks
Attitude towards own physical appearance
Attitudes towards the opposite sex, others in society, family and friends
Fighting manner: flight or fight
Conflict resolution (or lack thereof) manner
Sleep patterns:
(as in soundly vs. insomniac)
Morning or evening person:
Coffee or Tea (reg. or herbal):

angriest when:	Drink of choice (non-alcohol):
most bored when:	Dink of choice (alcohol):
most agitated when:	
most frightened when:	Phobias:
calmest when:	
funniest when:	Other personality traits

Journal Exercise

Enough sketching. Let's do some work.

Pick two characters you have created. Or feel free to create new characters. Create character inventories based on the character differentiation features, listed above. Feel free to add relevant categories.

Place your characters in the scenario below and have them interact. You will not use all inventory attributes in the scenario, and you may even discover things you don't know about your characters. The point is to get to know your characters well and, in knowing them, make them credible and interesting when they appear in your writing.

The Scenario

Your characters are the only two people in an elevator when the power goes out. The elevator is stuck for about 20 minutes. What do they do, how do they react, what do they say (or not say) to each other?

Feeling claustrophobic? Use the elevator scenario to see where your characters take you. Then feel free to put them into different situations to see how they react and evolve. For instance, you can have them stranded on the top of a mountain. (How did they get there? Is it important?) Or have them meet in a bar. Or perhaps they are working out beside each other at the gym. Or put them in bed together…

Try them in scenes that make sense, based on who they are. However, also put them into scenes that are totally out of character, so to speak, in terms of where you would expect to find them.

Keep the scenario to two characters; work on creating two distinct characters—each with their own voice and their own quirks. See if you can take two characters through a situation to a climactic moment.

Speaking of voice, try having them talk with no narrative interruption. Use dashes to distinguish changes in vocabulary, but don't use any "he said" or "she said" and don't

describe them in any way or describe any actions they might be taken. It would go something like this:
- Oh God, I don't believe it. I hope it's only temporary. I've got to get to the ninth floor by noon.
- I ride these elevators every day; this always happens.
- It happens every day?
- No, but often... It never lasts more than a minute. I can see by my Blackberry that it's 11:55. You should be fine.
- Can you put that in writing for me?
- No, but I can email it to you...

In this instance, see if you can move your characters through dialogue only to a climactic moment. And if that sounds vague, it is meant to sound vague. It's up to you to see where you go with it.

Have fun sketching with your characters, or sketching your characters. The work you do here will pay off when you have real characters coming into conflict in real situations—all in fictional stories.

Chapter 12: Show vs. Tell

Almost every writing student has heard this rule: *Show*, not *tell*. It's a solid rule, but the principle can be difficult to master.

Telling is the reliance on simple exposition:

Mary was an old woman.

Showing, on the other hand, uses evocative description:

Mary moved slowly across the room, her hunched form supported by a polished wooden cane gripped in a gnarled, swollen hand that was covered by translucent, liver-spotted skin.

Showing and telling as used above convey the same information—Mary is old. Telling states it flat-out. And showing? Read the example over and you will see it never states that Mary is old, yet leaves no doubt about it.

Now compare the two passages below.

Passage One

My father was cruel man. When I was a child, he often hurt me and caused me great pain. One day he beat me simply because I was crying.

Passage Two

The day I turned five I cried uncontrollably for some reason. I can't really recall why.

My father was deeply ensconced in the couch cushions, watching a football game and drinking beer. "Shut your friggin' yap, for christsake!" he shouted.

Maybe I was hungry; we had so little food then. Maybe I was sad because my mother had been in bed all day, again. For whatever reason, I continued to bellow. A second time my father shouted at me, but I cried on—an inconsolable prisoner in rickety, splintered wooden playpen prison.

A third time: "If you don't stop, right now," he said, and paused to take a deep swig of beer, "I will give you something to cry about."

I did not stop. I could not stop.

My father did not tell me a fourth time.

He turned and threw the half-empty beer bottle at me, hitting me flush in the temple and silencing me until long after the ambulance arrived and took me to the hospital...

In the second passage, I do not use the words "pain" or "hurt" or "cruel." But you see all of that and more. I suspect your reaction to the second passage is stronger that your reaction to the first because I am showing you what went on.

How Do You Apply Show vs. Tell?

First off, do not let the concept interfere with your creation. I tend to tell more than show in my first drafts. I don't want to get bogged down in the details of show. But I know some marvellous writers who can effortlessly paint word pictures in a first draft.

You will find your first draft or Freefall voice. If you lack show details, you can always look for opportunities to add them later. This is where the editor and creator work hand in hand. The editor finds the opportunities and then hands them off to the creator who expands a passage or writes a new one.

Do you remember *The Nuncles*? The details in that story were layered on over several drafts. If that is what it takes to get where you want to go, then that is what it takes.

Showing helps the reader see *your* images rather than filling in the blanks with their images. As you read your work over, look for opportunities to show. You do not have to show everything, but if you want to engage your reader and if you want your reader to see what you are writing, you have to show or create word pictures for the reader.

When reviewers use terms like "vivid," "evocative" or "cinematic" to describe a piece of prose, they really mean the writer has succeeded at showing, rather than merely telling.

Journal Exercises

1. With show vs. tell in mind, edit a Freefall (or several Freefalls). Look for opportunities to show rather than tell a couple of traits for each character, setting, situation or attitude in the work.
2. Pick one of your characters from your Character Differentiate work, and show him or her. Paint as vivid a portrait as possible of this person—age, body type, *and* personality, without using concrete words like "old" or "fat" or "dull".

3. Pick one of your Journey Through Childhood or Modelling exercises and rewrite it with show in mind. Look for opportunities to add details that will make the reader see what you see in your mind's eye.
4. Leave your computer behind. Take your writer's journal outside. Find a bench and gesture sketch all that you can see.
    a. If a car speeds by, don't tell us it was speeding. Show us.
    b. If you are in a park and can hear squirrels chattering, don't tell us they are chattering. Make us hear them.
    c. If you are in a café and the waiter is rude, don't tell us he (or she) was rude. Show us. And if the waiter is gorgeous or handsome, don't tell us, show us! Make us see what you see. And in that way we will feel what you feel as well.

Chapter 13: Elements of Poetry

In the last few chapters, we primarily looked at prose and the elements of fiction. In this chapter, we turn our attention to poetry. Let us define poetry:

> *Poetry is writing*
> *that formulates*
> *a concentrated*
> > *imaginative awareness*
> > *of experience in language*
> *chosen*
> > *and*
> > > *arranged*
> *to create a specific*
> *emotional response*
> *through meaning*
> *sound and rhythm...*

Okay, so I shaped Webster's definition, but I hope you get the picture.

In poetry, you create images with your words and you shape the lines for emphasis. By indenting the lines "imaginative awareness of experience in language", and by playing with "chosen and arranged" I am trying to draw your attention to these particular phrases—otherwise why treat them in a particular *visual* manner?

Notice also that Webster's definition mentions "sound" but says nothing about rhyme. While rhyme can be an integral part of poetry (see the excerpt from the T.S. Eliot poem below) it must work to enhance the sound, rhythm, and emotion—not detract from them as forced rhyme (rhyme for rhyme's sake) often does.

As with almost anything I say, there are exceptions. (*Now he tells me!*) There can be something awe-inspiring about a well-crafted sonnet that flows as smoothly as silk on skin even though it adheres to a rigid rhyming pattern. In limericks, forced rhymes are part of, and enhance, the humour. In nursery rhymes and the long odes of Homer and other classical poets, rhyme is used as a device to assist with memorization.

Words for Thought

If I feel physically as if the top of my head were taken off, I know that is poetry.
- Emily Dickinson.

You might agree, based on the way you were taught to explicate or interpret a poem—to search for meaning and the poet's true intent in seemingly obscure lines and images. That is, however, a completely different kind of taking your head off.

Emily Dickinson is talking about a powerful and wonderful feeling. Reading (and writing) poetry does not have to make your brain hurt. Poems do not have to be filled with obscure images and allusions. Doesn't mean they can't be; does mean they don't have to be.

Liberating Poetry

Poetry has moved from the strict structures of classical verse to free verse to modern poetry. At each step of the way, degrees of structure, form and decorum have been shed.

The French poets of the late nineteenth century—Rimbaud, Laforgue, Viele-Griffln and others—who, in their revolt against the tyranny of strict French *versification*, established the *Vers Libre* movement, from which the name *free verse* comes.

In the twentieth century, free verse has had widespread usage by most poets, of whom Rilke, St.-John Perse, T. S. Eliot, Ezra Pound, Carl Sandburg and William Carlos Williams are representative. Modern poetry originated in the 19th century, inspired by Ralph Waldo Emerson's call for poetic innovation and experimentation.

It is a long path from Homer's Iliad to Alan Ginsberg's *Howl* (if you have not read the latter, do try to find it) and all that follows. Some say *thank goodness poetry is liberated from form and structure*; others decry the loss of poetic decorum. I say, "Why take sides?" No matter its form, a crummy poem is a crummy poem and an excellent one is excellent.

In the Eye of the Beholder

What makes a poem crummy or excellent? As beauty is in the eye of the beholder, poetic excellence is best left to the ear (or mind) of the reader. However, I venture to say, that splendid poems speak in fresh and original ways and resonate on an emotional level with the reader.

With the caveat in mind, that there is a great deal of subjectivity involved when it comes to judging beauty, poetry or any literary or art form, allow me to excerpt a few lines from one of my favourite poems by T. S. Eliot, and to include two shorter poems for your review.

From "The Love Song of J. Alfred Prufrock"
Let us go then, you and I,
When the evening is spread out against the sky
Like a patient etherized upon a table;
Let us go, through certain half-deserted streets,
The muttering retreats
Of restless nights in one-night cheap hotels
And sawdust restaurants with oyster-shells:
Streets that follow like a tedious argument
Of insidious intent
To lead you to an overwhelming question...
Oh, do not ask, "what is it?"
Let us go and make our visit....

Read the above excerpt several times. Do you find it lyrical, almost song-like? (I'm not talking pop music lyrics here.) Do you find it rich in imagery? (Try to picture what an evening would look like if it were "spread out against the sky/Like a patient etherized upon a table.") Read it aloud. Notice how the rhythm changes, how the rhyme is integrated with the whole and how the absence of rhyme in places makes you pause, perhaps to ponder. Find the poem if you can (it's a much longer poem) and read it. There are many obscure images and allusions; trying to understand the poem might make your brain hurt. But don't let that spoil your reading of this exceptional poem.

The Café
by Leonard Cohen
The beauty of my table.
The cracked marble top.
A brown-haired girl ten tables away.
Come with me.
I want to talk.
I've taken a drug that makes me want to talk.

As with many modern poems, this is an internal monologue. Even the lines "Come with me. / I want to talk" are internal. The narrator does not say these lines aloud to the woman he is looking at. Although seemingly a simple poem, it paints a vivid picture: the poet sitting at a beautiful, cracked marble table longing to talk with a brown-haired woman ten tables away—I can see her, slightly out of focus, in the background of this poem. And what is this drug? An actual narcotic? Love? Lust? The desire/need to write poetry? Does it matter? Instead, ask yourself:

- Does the writing paint a picture and convey an emotion?
- Do I identify with the meaning of the poem; does the poem resonate within me?

The poet paints; the reader responds. On some levels, writing is that simple. Cohen's poem succeeds for me because I can see the picture he paints and because it resonates within me. Let me share the resonance with you: I am shy, but that has not stopped me from seeing people I would like to meet, to reach out to, to talk with. Although I find it difficult to overcome my shyness, the desire to do so (or the "drug") is still there. So I can relate to the poem because it expresses a feeling that I have—and does it well, poetically.

Finally, if I may, one last poem....

She Dances In The Open Air

By Paul Lima

She dances in the open air of Place Ville Marie
She dances to rock rhythms
as if enraptured by a sacred spirit
Her shrill voice shrieking
LIGHTMYFIRELIGHTMYFIRELIGHTMYFIRE OHYEAH
Her rainbow-coloured top
inching up her firm flat belly

She bumps and grinds as if drunk on electricity
Her thin arms flailing helplessly
A dervish whirling endlessly
As wolves around her howl incessantly

Until the music dies.

And I wonder where the evening
will disgorge her
And I hope the creatures
will be kind

I don't know if the poem works for you (it's all so subjective), but like *Kong*, this poem started off as Freefall. I was in Montreal. I saw this young girl dancing at a concert in a square. A local rock band was playing The Door's *Light My Fire*. The girl was dancing like a dervish. The image stayed with me; when I got back to my hotel, I began to Freefall in my journal. Sometime later, I was looking through my journal and discovered the Freefall. The image of her dancing still felt fresh. The Freefall opening line of "I saw her dancing in the open air at Place Ville Marie" became the opening line of the poem, and I went from there—shaping the poem from my Freefall. Why poetry instead of prose. I'm not sure. The scene just felt like poetry to me.

Writing Poetry

When writing poetry, don't force the rhyme and rhythm. Go with the flow and shape later—unless of course the poem demands that it be born with poetic shape as sometime happens.

A friend of mine once wrote 20 poems. Each one a gem. He did it over three days, just after his divorce came through. He did almost no revision. Many of them were published, they were that good. He hasn't written poetry since. They just came out because it was time for them to come out. It may happen again for him. It may not. He is not concerned.

If you want poetry to happen more than once in a blue moon, be prepared. Carry your journal with you. Write when you are inspired. If you don't create a poem immediately, do not despair. Put some time between you and your work, then go back to it and see if it still feels fresh. If so, work on it. Find the poetic essence; give your poem shape. Also, read it aloud. It helps. Poems should sing, even if you can't imagine musical accompaniment. It's a different kind of song. You'll know it when you hear it.

When editing, look at each word and phrase and ask yourself questions. Is there a more powerful way of saying this? Can I make this image more vivid? Do I need this word or phrase? What happens if it disappears? Will it be missed? How does the shape of the poem work with the words and phrases? How does shape augment meaning?

Edit the poem and revise the shape and make your poems as powerful as possible. Then put it away for at least a week or more. When you come back to it, see if it rekindles what you felt when you first wrote it. If so, you might have something there. If not, decide if it needs more work or if it was just a joyful writing exercise. Nothing wrong with that, and a lot right with it, if you ask me

Journal Exercise

Pick two of your previous Freefalls (Directed or Undirected; or write several new ones). When you are done, try to pare them down to their poetic essence. Add shape. Pare some more. Shape. Stop when you feel you are done, or your brain begins to hurt.

It never hurts to take some time off when editing; come back to a piece the next day feeling refreshed. When you come back to it, continue to revise and shape if you feel you can continue to boil the poem down to its poetic essence.

Other exercises you can try:
- Find inspiration in or model any of the poems above or other poems that seem to strike a chord with you.
- Go back to the Modeling chapter and rework a couple of poems that came out of the exercises there, or try to shape a modelling prose passage into a poem.

Note: If you feel that you are being asked to edit without a proper introduction to editing (in that we haven't looked at editing in detail) you are. It's good to plunge into things, to feel like you may be sinking only to find you can swim. That way, by the time we get to the chapter on editing you will feel as if you have an organic grasp of the editing process. Anything you pick up from that chapter will be a bonus.

Write Directed Freefalls using the lines below. When done, try to shape your Freefalls, or selected Freefalls, into poems; remove any words that do not belong; sharpen images.

- Rose, where did you get that red...
- The way she moved across the room...
- She moved like a comet racing against the night sky...
- I lost sight of him, but not before I lost my breath...
- When we parted, it was in...
- He did not die in the war, but...

A Final Note

Some people do not take to poetry. Others do. Some take a stab at it. Others avoid it. And still others find the poetry in their soul—some find it for a fleeting moment; others never lose it. Who is to say why it happens the way it happens.

With that in mind, I hope this chapter has inspired you to write a poem or poems. If not, no problem. Continue to Freefall daily and to work on your fiction. But be open to letting some of the elements of poetry work their way into anything you write.

Chapter 14: Critiquing and Editing

Getting Started

Rome wasn't built in a day. Few complete works of literature are either. This chapter will help you develop editing skills you can use to further polish some of the writing you have done while reading this book. But don't stop using Freefall and Clustering to help you create and plant new seeds.

Many of us have suppressed our spontaneous, child-like creative self for so long that we really enjoy making acquaintance with our inner creative being. Then, when introduced to our Editor, it's like meeting that grade five teacher we knew and perhaps loathed all over again.

You know the one. The one who made you write with a pencil when all the other kids in the class were using pens. Why did you have to use a pencil? Because your O's weren't round enough, you crossed your t's too high and your a's looked like e's. Or was it that your e's looked like a's.... And you couldn't spell worth a darn... At least that's my memory. That's who I equate my internal editor with. Or should I say, "That's with whom I equate my internal editor." You see, my internal editor constantly squawks: "Don't end sentences with prepositions! Brawwwk!"

Well, guess what? Both sentences are grammatically correct; the first sentence sounds far more natural. So now I end sentences with prepositions, when it feels appropriate, and cheerfully ignore my internal editor as she squawks away impotently.

Journal Exercise

Do you have an Internal Editor analogy? If one springs to mind, write about him/her/it. Write a Freefall that starts with:

"My internal editor reminds me of...."

Go. Do it. Have some fun. Before we get down to some serious editing information here.

A Reminder

Also, before we get into editing, I'd like to remind you that meeting your internal editor does not mean you suddenly give up on your creative self. Writing is still a *process*. Use your writer's journal as a safe place to Cluster and Freefall, to jot down ideas, to have fun, as a place to play with characters the way you might have played with dolls or toy soldiers when you were a wee bit younger than you are now....

In that spirit, here is another journal exercise you might want to try.

Journal Exercise

Sit in one room of your house or apartment and Freefall for about five minutes. Move to another room and Freefall for five minutes, then to another and repeat the pattern until you've written in every room or at least five different places... See what comes up.

You might continue the initial thread as you move from room to room or you might find that with a change of place comes a change of pace, topic, or whatever. Play with it.

A variation on this is to leave the house and write while in your yard, in a park, at a cafe, in library, at a gallery. Different places can help you tap into different streams of consciousness and develop different ideas. Try it. See what happens.

Having different writing exercises may help you develop the discipline required to write regularly, perhaps every day....

Editing Can be Daunting

Revising and editing can be daunting, intimidating even. However, it is an important part of the writing process—in its place. When editing, there's so much to look for—pacing, characterization, plot, theme, style, and so on—that a writer can get lost. When you sit down to write the first draft of a chapter or story, the jumble of clumsy words appearing on the screen is far from the perfect passages you'd imagined would come out. Experienced writers know that the jumble is not a problem because they realize that the more they revise the jumble, the closer they can bring it to their imagined state of perfection.

Fact is, the early drafts of a short story or novel lay down the foundation—the basic plot and characters; the final drafts fine-tunes what is there—building on the foundation and sometimes even reshaping it.

Early drafts are part of the discovery process, when the writing is most liquid. At this stage you feel free to add or delete passages, go in a different direction than intended, play with characters and so on. You are more daring because the story is still uncharted.

But once you have charted it—have the characters you want, doing and saying the things you want, in the order you want—you are ready to work on the final draft, or at least what feels like your final draft, before you start getting feedback from others on your work.

Editing: Before and After

Let's look at a passage before and after editing takes place.

Before

When promulgating your esoteric cogitations and articulating your amicable and philosophical observations beware of platitudinous ponderosity, and let your conversational communications possess a clarified conciseness and a compact comprehensibleness without coalescent consistency or a concatenated cogency. Eschew all conglomerations of flatulent garrulity, jejune babblement and asinine affectations and let your extemporaneous descantings have a voracious vivacity without rodomontade sagacity.

After

Speak briefly, say what you mean, mean what you say and, above all, don't use big words.

Sometimes the need for a thorough edit is fairly evident, no? While this kind of stuff looks like it came straight out of a Dilbert cartoon, you'd be amazed at the extent to which some internal corporate communications is virtually unintelligible due to the *utilization* (use) of *gargantuan* words where perfectly good small ones will do just fine, thank you. When writing, use your Thesaurus sparingly and try to avoid jargon. Jargon and the use of *colossal* (big) words usually stems from an attempt to impress readers, but generally has the opposite effect.

Having said that, I love the sound of the words *gargantuan* and *colossal*, whereas *big* is so dull, uninspired, unimaginative, bland... So the best advice I can give you is this: use words that are appropriate to the subject matter and audience. Also, make sure the words coming out of the mouth of your characters make sense, based on who the characters are and how they would communicate.

Speaking of Dilbert, here's an example from *The Dilbert Principle*, a book by Dilbert creator, Scott Adams:
- "I utilized a multi-tined implement to process a starch resource."
- <u>Translation</u>: "I used my fork to eat a potato."

Note on the Thesaurus

Many writers would not leave home without their Thesaurus. I do not blame them. I am not adverse (opposed, contrary, hostile) to using mine. However, just because a word shows up in a Thesaurus as a synonym for adverse, it does not make the word a correct substitute for adverse. Words have nuisances. Use of the right word often depends on context—as opposed to background, circumstance, situation, framework or milieu—if you get my drift.

Five Editor's Chores

Your internal editor has several basic chores:
1. To help your creator put flesh on the bones of your idea
2. To make sure the story—plot, characters, setting, narrative structure, tone and writing style—work together (in fiction)
3. To make sure the most suitable words and phrases are used
4. To ensure the writing sounds as potent or lyrical as it should (particularly in poetry)
5. To ensure the writing is technically accurate.

Although I've segmented the chores, frequently the editor does all this in one sitting. As you develop confidence in your creator and your editor, you will find them working in concert. Having said that, assign the first draft to your creator.

Chore One

To help your creator put flesh on the bones, the editor reviews your creative work and looks for themes, ideas or passages that might become stories or poems. The editor especially looks for recurring themes. Childhood is a recurring theme in this book. In your writing you might have many other recurring themes, such as loneliness, alienation, joy, love, friendship, betrayal. Relationships are often a recurring theme and there can be many thematic subsets within that theme.

When the editor finds a recurring theme, the editor smacks your creator on the side of the head and says, "Hey, do something with this. Cluster. Freefall. Paint word pictures. Do a character sketch. Put flesh on the bones. Give me something to work with." It's the creator's job to say, "You know Mr.-Grade-Five-teacher-who-tormented-me-all-my-life, you just might have something there... Now go away and let me have fun with this so as I can see what comes up."

After reading a Freefall and finding a potential story, I do a quick linear sketch: jot down the major characters, their relationship(s), the events that have unfolded and may yet unfold. I also try to find a place in my Freefall that feels like a good place to start. I especially try to find or create an opening line. Then I flip into Directed Freefall and write like heck until I feel I have reached some kind of resolution, conclusion, climax or simply drop from exhaustion.

If possible, I put this work (my "first draft") away for a while (at least 24 hours, sometimes a week or more) to let it steep and age before showing it to my editor to see if there is additional flesh we can add to the bones.

Chore Two

The editor makes sure the story—plot, characters, setting, narrative structure, tone and writing style—work together. To do so, the editor looks at the work from a broad perspective and asks (and answers) the following questions

- Does the story start where it should start?
- Does it end where it should end?
- Do the events connecting beginning to ending unfold in the most appropriate sequence?
- Who are the main characters?
- What are they like at the beginning of the story?
- What are they like by the end of the story?
- How do I feel about these characters as the story progresses? By the time I get to the end?
- Does each character have a distinct personality and voice?
- Do I care about these characters and the events that unfold?
- What events lead them to where they end up?
- Are the events credible? (Even science fiction and horror have to have what I would call a 'credible feel' to it.)
- Can I follow the story line from start to finish?
- Who is the narrator? What is the narrative voice?
- Does the narrative voice advance or interfere with the story?
- Where is the narrator in time and space?
- Where is the story set in time and space?
- Do I find the time, the time shifts, the setting and any setting changes credible?

- Do they add to the story?
- Has the story held my interest? Why? Why not?
- Is the writing style appropriate to the subject/topic/theme? Do they interfere with or facilitate the reading of the story?

At this point, the answers are handed back to the creator who goes away and works on the next draft. Using the editor's notes, the creator tries to make the story (or poem) as powerful and complete as possible. This may involve additional research, Freefalling or Clustering and, of course, writing.

Then the new work is returned to the editor for additional comments. Again, it helps to put the new work aside for a while, to let it steep, before going back and editing. **Note:** The editor might insist you go through this phase again. It can't hurt.

Chore Three

The editor has to make sure the most suitable words and phrases are used. This is generally done after attention has been paid to structure and other elements in Chore Two. It can be done at any time of course, but often it is done as a final line-by-line, word-by-word read during which the editor questions the use of each word or phrase, asking questions like:

- Is this the most potent word available?
- Am I using jargon or clichés?
- Does the tone/sound of this word best suit the subject matter?

Of course, you also want to make sure your editor does not replace perfectly good words or phrases with jargon, clichés or *enormously immense* words or phrases.

Chore Four

The editor ensures that the writing sounds as potent or lyrical as it should (particularly in poetry). This is a lot like chore number three. You are still looking for the best possible word, but you really want to make sure they sing. Remember the phrase *etherised on a table* from the TS Eliot poem? Sometimes such lyrical phrases can materialize out of Freefall. More often they are shaped over time, in collaboration between the creator and the editor.

How do you do it? Ah, if only I had the answer. It's a matter of looking, thinking, playing, substituting. It's perspiration and inspiration. And sometimes, it comes from leaving the bloody thing alone for a day, a week or longer and coming back to it refreshed so you can look at it with a more objectively critical eye.

I know a writer who reads his poems upside down and says he sees words that do not belong and somehow magically discovers the right word to use.

Some writers engage in guerrilla warfare, wherein they literally fight word by word through their poetry or fiction to make sure they kill the words that do not belong (or replace them with words that are allies of the work). Whatever works for you, the objective is the same: produce better (improved, healthier, superior, enhanced) writing.

Chore Five

To ensure that the writing is technically accurate. To do so, the editor does a line edit, reviewing line-by-line spelling and punctuation. As you may have noticed, I have broken some basic rules of grammar in this book—starting sentences with *but* or *and*, using sentence fragments. Ending sentences with prepositions. Things like that. Sometimes this can be done for effect. Sometimes it interferes with clarity. Make conscious decisions about when to break and when not to break the rules.

At this stage, I find it helps me edit if I do things like read my work aloud. I also read random paragraphs or stanzas out of context so I can focus on the words, phrases and sentences rather than the plot or logical flow. Some writers start at the last paragraph and work backwards one paragraph at a time. It helps them proofread for technical accuracy without the story getting in the way.

It also helps to have others read your writing. You get so close to it after several drafts that you can no longer see the little errors. I know that happens to me. (By the way, if you see any typos in this book feel free to email info@paullima.com and spell them out for me!)

I.C.E.: The Cold Way to Edit

Most editors I know have referred to themselves, at sometime or other, as "baby killers." A gruesome phrase, I confess. What editors mean is that they have had to kill the words and phrases (the babies) their writers were most in love with (and couldn't kill themselves). If you find yourself looking at your writing saying, "Oh, how cute!" It could be a sign that you have a baby that needs to be tossed out. But don't toss out the bath water (the story) with the baby! When editing, you have to be I.C.E. cold. Look at each paragraph in your story, or each word and line in your poem, and...

- **Improve**: use the most appropriate word and make sure your writing—grammar and spelling—is technically accurate

- **Cut**: omit unnecessary or redundant words and phrase; beware of words or phrases you find yourself admiring
- **Expand**: review Clusters and Freefalls or first drafts. Expand by adding pertinent information or necessary details required to flesh out a character, plot, meaning... <u>Sounds easy, yes?</u> It takes work: a combination of thought and experimentation because, when writing, the possibilities seem endless. Editing comes quite naturally to some; others would rather sit in a tub full of worms than edit. Either way, editing is part of the process. If you have difficulty editing, consider taking a night school or online editing courses (unless you can afford to pay someone to edit for you). The fact is, most published authors have editors. (I've had two editors look at this book, and probably could have used a third!)

The best advice I can give you, though, is <u>read</u>. For instance, if you do not know how to structure/punctuate dialogue, read. See how published authors do it. If you read a lot, you will see that there is the way your teachers told you:

"How do you structure and punctuate conversation?" Terry asked Mr. Smith.

"This is how you do it," Mr. Smith replied.

"Thank you!"

"You are welcome," Mr. Smith said. "You are most welcome."

But you need to know, that is not the only acceptable way of doing it! Read and you will see other ways of structuring and punctuating conversations.

Journal Exercise

I don't know what more to say about editing. Review the editor's chores and apply them to some of what you have written. Beyond that, you might want to join a writer's workshop. In workshops, you read your work aloud and other participants give you feedback.

Local libraries sometimes organize workshops (or you will see posters for them in libraries or on college and university campuses). Or check online and see if you can find local writing workshops.

You can also show your work to friends or relatives. Let them know you are looking for feedback. The hope is you will get constructive comments you can think about and apply if they seem useful. But remember, you might receive comments that feel hurtful and remind you of my grade five teacher (I mean *remind you of your internal editor*). So, if you feel like going public in your quest to find editing assistance, make sure you wear your *thick skin coat*. You cannot control what others will say. All you can do is listen and filter the remarks. Apply constructive remarks; discard destructive.

Summing Up

By this point in the book, you have planted many seeds, drawn many gestures. Some of your seeds may be blooming. Some of your lines may have taken shape. Read this chapter, pick one seed or line (Freefall or other work you have created) and revise/edit it.

If you are working on a short story, the opening chapters to a novel or a collection of poems, take some time to get to the point where you feel the work is done. It can take time!

How will you know when you are through editing? I wish there was a simple answer. It's not like baking a cake: An hour in the oven at 400 degrees and it's done. Getting feedback from others might help. Putting the work away for a week or so after you have revised it, and then looking at it again and asking all of the questions above might help. At some point, you just have to call it *done*—especially if it is going to be published. But maybe years from now, you might revise it again. I know I have revised work years after calling it done.

Such is the writing life.

Chapter 15: Leading Up to Something

Leads are important. They draw the reader into your work. They set the tone for all that follows. Many book buyers read the first few paragraphs or pages of a book and buy (or do not buy) based on the lead.

Take a moment and read the three leads below (one of which you have already read) before you read why they are here.

From Tom Clancy's *Shadow Watch*

Later, when it became both her job and obsession to determine what happened at the pad, she would remember how everything had gone just right until it all went terribly wrong, turning excitement and anticipation into horror, and forever changing the course of her life. Astronaut, media celebrity, role model, mother—the world's easy reference tags for her would remain the same. But she knew herself well. There was the Annie Caulfield who had existed before the disaster, and the Annie Caulfield who eventually arose from its ashes. They were two very different women.

From Diane Baker Mason's *Last Summer at Barebones*

I go back to Barebones Lake the Wednesday before the Saturday on which I plan to shoot my sister.

The road lopes through the woods, there only by the grace of the forest's indulgence, and the car rides it bareback, spitting gravel from its tires at the turns. At the wheel of the car is me, instead of the Dad, and it's a sporty Mazda instead of a cumbersome, fishtailing Vistacruiser wagon. My Mazda has a CD player, and a LED digital display for its gauges, the wagon had dials with pointed needles that glowed phosphorescent in the dusk, and a pushbutton radio which, north of Severn River, only brought in static.

It's thirty years since I spent those seven summers on the island. The last was the summer before I turned fourteen....

From Paul Lima's *The Conquest of Kong*

It was on the congested grounds of the Canadian National Exhibition that Father conquered the world-famous ape. The glassy-eyed creature, wearing a New York Yankee baseball cap, glared down at the midway masses from his perch in the Strike Out tent. I sometimes wonder how we must have appeared from Kong's vantage point—my brawny father with premature flecks of grey dotting slicked-back waves and his scrawny kid with the bristled brush cut.

Above the crowd the titanic brute, the most coveted prize at the CNE, seemed unconquerable.

Now What?

What did you think? Did you notice any similarities between the three leads? If not, go back and read them again. Read *analytically*.

What do you find out in each lead?

I won't keep you in *suspense*... for too long.

First, let me say, they are all about completely different topics, subject and people. No doubt about that. If you were at all intrigued by the lead of *Shadow Watch*, I'm sorry to say that the rest of the novel is a major disappointment. But what a lead! "Later." What a great first word. To start a novel with what happens later? And what impact what happens later will have on Annie?

Last Summer at Barebones lives up to the expectations it creates. The question is: Were you hooked by the lead? Do you think she kills her sister? The only way you are going to find out is by reading the book, no?

And you've already read *The Conquest of Kong*. Now analyse the lead. What does the title tell you? What does the first paragraph tell you? Is the father going to conquer Kong? Do you see where I am going with this?

None of these leads could have been written without the author knowing what was going to happen "later...."

The first word of the Clancy's novel is not "Now" or "Previously" but a word that alludes to the future. As reader, you know from the first line that something happened and that it is going to *change* (Delta factor) "Annie Caulfield who had existed before the disaster, and the Annie Caulfield who eventually arose from its ashes." You already know that the two Annies "were two very different women."

The question is: Do you want to go for the journey to see how and why Annie changes? That is the question, I put to you, that all readers ask:

Do I want to go on the journey to see if anything happens?

Before an author can start a novel or short story with a lead that foreshadows the outcome, the author has gone on the journey. The first several drafts are the author's journey. If you do not finish the first draft and get to some place called "the end" how are you ever going to start your story? You have to know your destination before you can figure out where to start so you can plot a route to get you from beginning to end.

Look at Mason's opening again: "I go back to Barebones Lake the Wednesday before the Saturday on which I plan to shoot my sister." Mason has to know what is going to happen to write a lead like that. Do you want to go on the journey and find out if the main character does what she plans to do?

Look at the transition sentence, the sentence that takes you out of the lead and into the story: "It's thirty years since I spent those seven summers on the island. The last was the summer before I turned fourteen...." The journey begins there. We will find out what happened that summer; not doubt it will tell us why she plans to kill her sister.

As Mason told me in an interview: "I had no idea what was going to happen when I started this novel. It wasn't until I found out what was going to happen, that I could come back and write the beginning of the novel." Once she reached her destination, she could go back and begin her journey. Yes, she had to start somewhere in her first draft before she could reach her destination. But that does not mean she could not go back and revisit/revise her beginning once she reached her destination.

Again, let us look at *The Conquest of Kong*:

It was on the congested grounds of the Canadian National Exhibition that
Father conquered the world-famous ape.

Sentence one tells us that Father conquers Kong, does it not? So why bother to build to this: "Above the crowd the titanic brute, the most coveted prize at the CNE, seemed *unconquerable*." Does that not pose the question: Do you want to go on the journey to see how Father conquered something that seemed unconquerable? It is as simple as that.

However, and I suspect you know this already, the story is about *more* than Father conquering Kong, is it not? Is it not about a boy and his father developing a bond that, the reader learns, was not there at the beginning? Is it not about *change*? Just as Mason's story will be about more than one sister shooting or not shooting another. There will be change.

Clancy's story should have been about Annie changing. In fact, it is about so much—

much of it not relating to Annie at all—that the novel loses focus or a sense of purpose. But still, *what a brilliant lead!*

Find Endings

The exercises in this book have given you many starts. Your task now is to select some of your starts and find ways of pushing them towards a destination that is not yet known. Go back to some of your work and ask yourself: "What happens next? Why? And then? Why?" Carry on until you reach something that feels like an "end." Once you arrive at your destination, ask yourself the *big* question:

Now that I know where I am going, where should I begin?

That does not mean you will begin your story by alluding to or reflecting the end or some sense of change. There are many, many ways to begin. (Read other stories and novels analytically to find other ways and places to begin your stories.) It does mean, however, that you will begin your story where your story should begin. Where is that? Only your heart and mind (and a lot of analytical reading) can tell you. Then the work really begins. It becomes your job to make the journey truly worthwhile. For yourself. And the reader.

And in the End…

Speaking of destinations, how do you end a story? After all, it is—ultimately—the end that we are leading up to.

First of all, make sure you have completed at first draft, even if you feel you really haven't discovered where the story is supposed to end, before you do any significant editing. In other words, push it to someplace that feels like it could be the end or at least sort of finished. Then take time off to think.

A story needs a resolution—a climax and denouement. Now a deliberate lack of a resolution can be a resolution, so your story doesn't have to be tied up all neatly in a bow. But you do have to look back and ask yourself: who is/are the central character(s). What is/are the central issue(s). How is it (are they) resolved (or not resolved)?

If you don't have that at the end of your story, close your eyes and visualize it. What is the main issue, the central conflict of the story? How is it (or should it be) resolved (or not resolved)? Who is involved in the resolution? What do they do or say or think or feel (or all of the above) in order to reach that point of resolution (or understanding that there will be no resolution)? Open you eyes and write what you saw….

Once you have that ending down, reflect on it. Again, close your eyes…

Where do you see your protagonist at the very end of all this, after the resolution—maybe minutes or days or weeks or years afterwards? Why? How does she, he or they get there? Is there a path in the story leading beyond the resolution to that place? Where is that place? Why is that place? What is that place: a state of being, of understanding, a physical place, an internal or external place? Visualize it, and then write. Put your protagonist there (with any other significant characters that should be there at the end) and write them into being.

Now all this might feel *tacked on*. But once you have that ending (climax and denouement), ask yourself if this is where you want the story to end, the place the journey takes you, the reader and your characters. And ask yourself if all that comes before the ending leads you to the end? If not, you have two options:

- Revise the path/journey so it gets you to the ending you want
- Revise the ending so it is somewhere that the story leads to.

Ending Exercise

All that is fine in theory, but there is something you can do—beyond thinking and visualizing—to help you discover your story ending. Remember the *Delta factor* exercise in Chapter 4?

In that exercise, you copied your lead—your first paragraph or first several paragraphs—and pasted it on to the end of the story.

When you do this, you have the beginning of your story at the end. Then you ask yourself: What has changed from where this story began? With that in mind, you edit, revise or otherwise hack away at the beginning that you have pasted at the end of your story, and turn it into the ending. It might not look anything like the beginning when you are through with it, and that's okay. All that matters is that you know and understand how and why you got to the end, and that it makes sense to the story.

Then, of course, you go back to the beginning and see if, based on the ending, you should revise where your story opens. The circle is all part of the process of making the story as focused and complete as possible.

Chapter 16: Thoughts on Marketing

So far in this book, we've looked at the lonely part of the writer's life: research, creation and editing. These are, for the most part, solitary activities (although you may show your work to other writers for feedback to help you with editing or you may workshop a solid draft of your work). If you're like me, you love the solitude. It's one of the reasons why you write.

When it comes to <u>marketing</u> your work, you start to communicate with a limited public (agents and/or publishers). Of course, there is the potential you may soon be communicating, through your words, with a larger public—if your book is published. Depending on what you write and who publishes you, this may be a limited or specialized audience or a larger, mass audience.

There are two basic approaches to marketing work:
- Submitting unsolicited manuscripts
- Querying (pitching ideas).

Unsolicited Manuscripts

What does submitting an unsolicited manuscript mean? It means you write your novel, short story, poems (or how-to book or other non-fiction book, articles, script, etc), and submit the finished manuscript, with a cover letter to an agent, book publisher, magazine or newspaper editor or film producer.

Since the person to whom you submit your work has not requested (solicited) the submission, this is called submitting an <u>unsolicited manuscript</u>.

This approach is usually reserved for submitting short stories and poetry to literary magazines, letters to newspaper and magazine editors, and personal essays to magazines or op-ed (opposite the editorial page) pieces to newspapers. It is also used occasionally when submitting articles to magazines and newspapers—most frequently by new writers.

Most magazines and newspapers state in their mastheads (the place where you find the publication's editor, address, email address, web site, phone number, etc.) whether they accept unsolicited manuscripts. If they don't accept them and you submit an unsolicited manuscript, it <u>will not be read</u>.

However, our focus here is on submitting a novel, collection of short stories or poems to an agent or publisher. Although email is so convenient, if you want to submit an unsolicited manuscript, I recommend you use the mail. (Never submit an unsolicited manuscript by email unless you know for sure the editor or publisher accepts email submissions.) If you want your work returned when submitting an unsolicited manuscript, include a SASE (self-addressed, stamped envelope) otherwise you'll never see it again.

These days, not seeing your work again is not such a big deal because most people have computers and can reprint manuscripts. But if it's a 350-page novel, you may not want to reprint it! If you don't want your work back, leave out the SASE and state "Do Not Return Manuscript" in your cover letter so the editor knows you have not accidentally forgotten to enclose the SASE.

Before you do anything, though, check the website of the agent or publisher to find out if they accept unsolicited manuscripts. Some don't. Some don't want the whole novel or book; they may only want a cover letter and the first three chapters.

Why Submit Unsolicited Material?

Why would a writer research, create and edit a work then submit it not knowing if the editor or publisher wants to publish it? For most literary work (short stories, poetry) there is no alternative. It's how literary magazines or e-zines (electronic magazines) work. There is no point in pitching a story idea. The editor is interested in your writing, not in your ability to write a query letter that outlines your idea.

When it comes to getting non-fiction articles published, new writers are concerned editors won't buy articles based on ideas because new writers have limited writing experience. The new writer hopes the editor will like the article and will buy it, no matter how limited the writer's experience.

And when it comes to novels, unless you have a track record—have published a number of short stories in literary magazines or have previously published a novel—submitting an unsolicited manuscript (or the first three chapters of your manuscript) is the only way you can get it into the hands of an agent or publisher.

Querying (Pitching Ideas)

When should you query (pitch an idea)? You generally pitch article ideas to newspapers and magazines, especially when the publication's website says: "Unsolicited manuscripts not accepted." Also, when it comes to book publishers (or agents) and non-fiction work (how-to, reference, training, biographies, etc.), it is best to query first with a proposal and synopsis of your book.

In fact, I would suggest you not even start to write a non-fiction book unless you have lined up an agent or publisher—unless you are willing to self-publish which is definitely a low-cost or even no-cost option (see the chapter on self-publishing and print on demand later in this book).

The query letter is the classic way of selling editors or publishers on your idea *and* on your ability to write an article or book based on your idea. Pitch first, do all the research and writing later—once you know you're going to be paid. Makes sense to me!

For newspaper or magazine articles, a query is a one- or two-page letter addressed to the editor outlining:
- Your idea;
- Why you should be the one to write the article;
- Why readers would want to read it.

When it comes to non-fiction books, book publishers need detailed proposals that include:
- A synopsis of the book's central idea
- The target audience (managers, stamp collectors, do-it-yourself web page designers, etc.)
- The reasons why you have the ability to complete the project
- Three sample chapters (optional)
- A brief biography.

Where to Pitch/Submit

"Where should I pitch my books of fiction or poetry?" I am asked this question often. The answer, vague I'm afraid, is: *it depends.*

First off, if you are trying to get a short story or poem published, I suggest you go online to Google (www.google.com) and type in literary e-zine, e-zine, electronic magazine, writing markets or other related words into the search box. A whole world of potential markets will open up to you.

Beware of any websites that want to charge you a fee to publish your work, especially if they want you to buy a pile of your books. While they will publish your work, the distribution (getting it into bookstores) is then left up to you. That is a difficult and expensive part of publishing. If you want to self-publish, you can probably cut a deal with a printer and save yourself a lot of money or you can use print on demand (discussed later in this book).

Beware also of any editors who offer to edit your work and promise they will get it published. They may be working in cahoots with a vanity publisher. That does not mean you should never pay someone to edit or help you edit your work, but investigate their motivation and business ties first.

Before submitting fiction or poetry to a magazine or e-zine, <u>read back copies of the magazine</u> or e-zine. Make sure the work you are submitting fits the mandate, tone and style of the magazine.

Before submitting your novel to a publisher or an agent, <u>read some of the titles</u> the publisher has published or the agent has represented. Make sure the work you are submitting falls within the range of the kind of work the company publishes or the agent represents. For instance, you wouldn't send a sci-fi or horror novel to Harlequin Romance Publications, would you? Seems obvious? But you'd be surprised at how many people do!

When it comes to formatting your manuscript, check the agent's or publisher's website to see if they have any suggestions. If you don't see any suggestions, simply set up your page in Word (or whatever word processor you use) to 8-1/2 by 11", with a one-inch margin (top, bottom and left/right). On the cover page, include your book title, name and contact information. Double-space the body of your work. You can indent each paragraph or simply put an extra space between each paragraph—as I have done here.

Finally, include the book title and page number in the header on each page. If you don't know how to do the formatting outlined here, consider taking a course in Word or looking up how-to online. It can't hurt to know how to manipulate pages in your word processor.

Finally, I admit that it is not easy to find an agent who can represent your work to a publisher or to find a publisher who will read, let alone publish, your work. Do yourself a favour—don't get hung up on this until you have completed a solid first draft of a manuscript and worked on a couple of revisions. Also, see if you can get shorter work published in online or print literary publications.

As you move forward with your writing, remember what William Forrester, the reclusive writer in the novel *Finding Forrester* (by James W. Ellison) says to his young protégé: "You write your first draft with your heart. You write your second draft with your head."

Publishing your work is also all about the head; whatever you do, don't lose heart! Remember how long it took Diane Baker Mason to become a novelist. So don't let the process of looking for a publisher spoil your love of writing—otherwise, you will have to re-rediscover the joy of writing!

We have covered a great deal in a short chapter here. However, I find most people are here because they want to kick-start their writing. If you are interested in pursuing publishing opportunities, you may have questions this chapter has not answered. There are other books, courses, workshops that can help you, and you might be interested in the chapter in this book on print on demand (POD) or self-publishing.

Chapter 17: Bonus Exercises

To help you move forward, there are a series of bonus writing exercises. I hope these additional exercises will inspire you to continue to write.

1. Describe your thoughts or feelings about religion in a letter that begins: "Dear God (or address it to whomever your deity may be)...."
2. It's Groundhog Day! Will the sun come out on your writing or will you have six more weeks of cold starts? Write about how you feel about writing right now.
3. Have a conversation with a child about anything of interest to that child. Then, recreate your conversation in a scene that includes dialogue and setting.
4. Take your emotional temperature as you read the daily newspaper. Write a response to the story, article, photograph or letter that evokes the most heat, and send a letter to the editor. Freefall it, then I.C.E. edit it. *pg. 90*
5. Do you know someone who is hard to understand or who you just can't "read"? Write a short piece about what you really think goes on in that person's head. Become that person. Write in first person, starting with "I..."
6. Did you have or do you have a best friend who you admired? Write a note to this person and describe what you admire(d) most about him or her.
7. Describe your dream car or dream vacation on paper. Who would be in the car or on the holiday with you? Where would you go? What would you do once you arrived?
8. The smell of your favourite homemade cookie or a certain someone's musky perfume is hard to forget. Write down five memorable smells and the time in your life that you associate with them. Describe the emotion the scent evokes. Now create a scene in which this scent exists. Who is there? What is going on? Push it into fiction. Or Cluster the word "scent" or "aroma" and Freefall.
9. Valentine's Day! Write a heartfelt love letter to your significant other or an imaginary lover—without using the word "love."
10. Let God (or your deity) reply to your Freefall (exercise #1, above).
11. Write a dialogue between yourself today and yourself of 10, 15 or 20 years ago. Or have your present self write your past self a letter. Have your past self reply.

Write at least 10 letters between the two of you.

12. Are you always satisfied with the fortunes you receive from fortune cookies? Write your own fortune. When that is done, write a story about a fictional person who receives this fortune, and what impact it has on that person when it comes true.
13. Revel in the atmosphere of the season by looking out of a window for a few minutes. Expand on what you see and how it makes you feel, in a brief reflective essay or short fiction piece. Then take two characters that have come out of previous work and put them outside your window, in the scene. Answer in your head: What is there relationship? Why are they there? What are they talking about? Where have they come from? Where are they going? Then write...
14. What is your favourite recipe or dish? Can you cook, or are you horrible at it? Write about cooking.
15. Write an epitaph or obituary, perhaps your own.
16. Write a fictional epitaph or obituary. Then give the person a name, gender, age, date of birth, date of death, birthplace. Where was the person when he or she died? How did he or she die? Who is attending the funeral? Who is not there (who one might think should be there)?

Write a story that starts with the above epitaph or obituary. After writing down the epitaph or obituary, flashback to the beginning of the character's life and outline in point form the significant details of that person's life from start to finish. Freefall from point to point-to-point until you reach the end–and the epitaph or obituary, the reason for those particular words, comes clearly into focus.

And Don't Forget...

Freefall daily. Cluster on a regular basis. Plant many seeds. Cultivate the ones that feel like they deserve or require your attention. May many stories and poems bloom!

All the best with your writing!

Chapter 18: Sentences and Paragraphs

Those of you who may need some help writing clear and concise sentences and effectively structuring paragraphs will find this quick primer on writing sentences and paragraphs of interest. If you want to spend more time improving your writing, especially if you are involved in business writing or write non-fiction, consider buying *Harness the Business Writing Process* (available mid-2009). You can read more information online at www.paullima.com/books or email the author at info@paullima.com.

Active versus Passive Voice

When it comes to sentences, writers should be aware of several elements. One of the most important is voice. There are two voices—the passive voice and the active voice. I promise I am not going to get all grammatical on you; however, I have to use three grammatical terms—subject, object and verb.

In the active voice, the subject acts upon the object. The action is described by the verb. As in: *The dog bit the boy.*

"The dog" is the subject, "bit" is the verb and "the boy" is the object. In the passive voice, the sentence starts with the object receiving the action, so this form is much more indirect, as in: *The boy was bitten by the dog.*

Notice the active voice is more dynamic. Also, it takes fewer words to write a sentence using the active voice. This leads to another important aspect of writing: generally, concise writing is easier to read and more easily understood.

Often, a passive sentence doesn't even contain a subject so the person or thing responsible for the action isn't even mentioned. This is why politicians and lawyers often use the passive voice.

Passive voice is not grammatically incorrect. It isn't very concise, however, and can be vague or confusing. Consider the following:

Passive: You were asked by me to submit your expense report by the middle of the month.

Active: I asked you to submit your expense report by the middle of the month.

Passive: Your payment was received two days late by us, which caused delays.

Active I: We received your payment two days late, which caused delays.
Active II: You sent the payment two days late, which caused delays.

Make sure your grammar checker is set up to detect the passive voice. When grammar checker stops at a passive sentence, ask yourself if using active voice would improve it. You don't have to convert all passive voice sentences to active voice. However, make a conscious choice to convert or leave them.

Speaking of sentences, a complete sentence requires a subject and a verb (action): "I laughed."

"I" is the subject. "Laughed" is the verb. But two-word sentences don't always cut it in writing. So that's when we add the third component—the object, as in: *The boy kicked the ball.*

"The boy" is our subject (the person who does the action). "Kicked" is the verb or action. "The ball" is our object; it receives the action. I call these three elements—subject, verb and object—the heart of the sentence.

If you ever feel that your sentences are getting too complex, find the heart. Once you have identified the heart, you can expand your sentence logically, while keeping the meaning clear.

For instance, where did the ball go when the boy kicked it?

The boy kicked the ball through the window.

What happened to the window?

The boy kicked the ball through the window, which shattered into a thousand pieces.

Tell me more about this boy and the ball that he kicks:

The tall, thin Caucasian boy kicked the blue soccer ball through the window, which shattered into a thousand pieces.

Our sentence is becoming longer and more complex, yet it is easy to understand because we are building around the heart of the sentence. Now imagine this action was committed by a criminal and the homeowners had an alarm system.

The tall, thin, armed and dangerous Caucasian boy kicked the blue soccer ball through the window, which shattered into a thousand pieces and caused the alarm to sound, notifying the security company, which dispatched its agents to the scene of the crime.

Writing Concisely

Whether you are writing fiction or non-fiction, you can pack a lot into a sentence if you identify the heart and build around it. However, just because you can pack a lot into a sentence does not mean you should. This can make your sentence long, convoluted and confusing. In addition, if all your sentences were constructed in a similar manner, your writing could become a tad tedious to read.

So vary the voice and length of your sentences. However, be aware of wordy writing. Wordy writing sacrifices readability and coherence (passive voice can contribute to wordiness). Your goal is to write concise sentences that clearly convey the meaning that you intend them to convey. In other words, write concisely, but not at the expense of meaning.

> *To write concisely, please consider removing unnecessary, extraneous, redundant and repetitive words, phrases, clauses and sentences, without sacrificing appropriate detail.*

Of course, if the sentence were written concisely, it would read:

> *To write concisely, remove unnecessary words, phrases, clauses and sentences, without sacrificing appropriate detail.*

Notice how we removed the "please consider" and changed "removing" to "remove." There may be times in your writing when you want to be less direct to encourage the reader to consider various options. However, if you are a subject expert and if something should be done in a particular way to be effective, say so and remove the qualifiers, such as "please" and "consider"—as we have done in the second version of the sentence. It is not impolite to write bluntly.

And hey, if the reader does not want to do what you suggest, the reader does not have to do it!

It is, on the other hand, possible to be too concise. Think about this version of the sentence:

> *To write concisely, remove unnecessary words, without sacrificing appropriate detail.*

One might argue it is redundant to use "words, phrases, clauses and sentences." However, each is a different part of speech and you may want to identify each one of them because concise writing doesn't just mean removing unnecessary words. Sometimes it requires you to remove phrases, clauses, entire sentences and perhaps even the occasional paragraph.

In short, when giving instructions, be as specific as possible so the reader understands you. Remember, your readers are not a homogeneous mass. Some might get what you mean right away; others might need a bit more information. If you remove all the unnecessary, extraneous, redundant and repetitive information, you can include a tad more appropriate information that some readers might need, without sacrificing conciseness.

In other words, don't write like the bureaucrat would write:

We are less than pleased due to the fact that it is, at this point in time, the season of winter.

Instead, write like Shakespeare:

"Now is the winter of our discontent."–Richard III

At the same time, you don't have to be Shakespeare to be an effective non-fiction or fiction writer. You just have to be clear and concise.

Having said all that, fiction and poetry often breaks the rules of grammar or of conventional writing and sentence structure. If you made James Joyce or Joseph Conrad write concisely, you would have eradicated two literary geniuses! I am not advocating that you attempt to write your fiction like Joyce or Conrad; nor am I suggesting that you be a dry business writer. Heck, we saw how the business bureaucrat would ruin a wonderfully poetic Shakespearian line.

What I am suggesting is this: if you want to break the rules, make sure you know them first. And don't just break them for the sake of breaking them. Do so for specific effect—to somehow make a character seem more real, to paint a more vivid scene or to build suspense or mystery.

How to Structure a Paragraph

Being clear and concise doesn't just apply to sentences. It also applies to paragraphs. Paragraphs perform three main functions:

- Develop the unit of thought stated in the paragraph's topic sentence, which states the paragraph's main idea.
- Provide a logical break in material, which signals a new aspect of the topic or a new topic.
- Create a visual break on the page, which makes the document easier to read.

You can put your topic sentence at the beginning of the paragraph, as in this example of business writing:

The cost of training new Customer Service Representatives is significant. The organization must cover the price of classroom facilities, instructors, manuals and employee salaries during the three-week training period.

Notice the main topic is the "The cost of training..." sentence. You could replace "of training new Customer Service Representatives" with "of printing documents" or "of heating the office" or any other significant cost the reader needs to know about. In this instance, the topic is "The cost of training new Customer Service Representatives is significant."

You can, on occasion, place your topic sentence at the end of the paragraph. Doing so varies your writing style. It also lets you build up to the topic sentence with a bit of dramatic flourish. This can be effective, as long as it is not overused. Here is an example, with the topic sentence in bold at the end:

Energy does more than make our lives more comfortable and convenient. It enables us to prosper. The proof? The surest and quickest way to reverse economic progress would be to cut off the nation's oil resources. The country would plummet into the abyss of economic ruin. ***In short, our economy is energy-based.***

In the above paragraph, we have dramatically built up to our topic sentence. This can be quite effective. However, if you do this too often your writing will become tedious.

Now let's look at some fiction:

It was on the congested grounds of the Canadian National Exhibition that Father conquered the world-famous ape. The glassy-eyed creature, wearing a New York Yankee baseball cap, glared down at the midway masses from his perch in the Strike Out tent. I sometimes wonder how we must have appeared from Kong's vantage point—my brawny father with premature flecks of grey dotting slicked-back waves and his scrawny kid with the bristled brush cut. Above the crowd the titanic brute, the most coveted prize at the CNE, seemed unconquerable.

Notice how the first line of the story established the location and introduces two characters—if you count Kong as a character. It also introduces the narrator and the topic of the story—the conquest. The second sentence describes Kong, who was introduced in the first sentence, and makes Kong look ominous. Then it shifts points of view—giving the reader a look at our narrator and his father from Kong's perspective. And it ends with both the CNE, which was introduced in the first sentence, and the conquest, of sorts, by using the word *unconquerable*. In short, the first sentence serves as the topic sentence for the paragraph and, in many ways, for the short story.

The second sentence enlightens the reader about the relationship between the boy and his father: the boy had never been to the Ex with his father. And notice how, even though the flat is full of stuffed animals won at the Ex, the boy has only heard about how they were won from a third party. So the focus here is about the alienation between the son and the father, which has been introduced in the first sentence:

> *I had never been to the Ex with my father. Although stuffed snakes, poodles, giraffes and bears populated our cramped flat, I had only heard about his midway triumphs from Ted McMaster who owns the garage where Father works. Ted told me that my father had once been addicted to midway games.*

One final comment about paragraphs. Look for opportunities to use bullet points or numbered points. Although they are not used often in fiction, stay open to using them if it seems appropriate. Used properly, bullets or numbers let you convey an idea in a manner that is easier for your readers to scan, read and understand. If they are overused, they can make your document look like it lacks focus or emphasis.

Here is an example of a sentence that would benefit from a numbered list:

> *To start juggling, you must first pick up "A" in your right hand, then you should pick up "B" in your left hand, and then you should toss "A" and then "B" into the air, catching "A" as you toss "B" and catching "B" as you toss "A." Repeat continuously.*

Let's see it as a list:

> To start juggling:
> 1. Pick up "A" in your right hand;
> 2. Pick up "B" in your left hand;
> 3. Toss "A" into the air;
> 4. Toss "B" into the air while catching "A";
> 5. Toss "A" back into the air while catching "B";
> 6. Repeat continuously.

After reading the numbered list, you know how to juggle. Well, not quite. However, the instructions are easier to follow because your eye pauses at the end of each point so you better understand the steps involved in juggling.

Again, in fiction, it could be argued that you would seldom if ever use bullet points or number point. Be aware of them and use them when and where it makes sense.

Chapter 19: A Tale of Self-Publishing

Could traditional book publishers be heading the way of traditional music companies, which are heading the way of dinosaurs, thanks to the Internet? They could, but for different reasons.

People are not endangering the publishing industry by downloading books for free over the Internet, not the way pirated music downloading continues hurt the music industry. However, many authors are eschewing traditional publishers in favour of online print-on-demand (POD) companies. This is costing publishers authors. In addition, many of these books are available electronically, making the print industry redundant.

I am one of the many authors using POD.

When I first approached a traditional Canadian publisher with my how-to book about freelance writing, *The Business of Freelance Writing*, I received tentative interest. However, the publisher wanted to know if I could guarantee 2,000 sales of the book through seminars or writers' associations. If so, the publisher was willing to print 4,000 copies and put the other 2,000 into circulation. This was not a vanity publisher. It was a legitimate publisher of popular fiction and non-fiction titles.

I could not guarantee the sales and was not willing to buy that many books to flog at my writing seminars, so I approached another publisher. However, by the time the second publisher replied (with a "no thanks"), I had discovered Lulu.com, an online POD company.

Just as some music groups are selling CDs from their websites—cutting out music companies, distributors, and retailers—literally tens of thousands of self-published authors have cut out the middlemen and now sell self-published books online. Lulu.com says it has 1.2 million registered users and receives about 4,000 pieces of new content—books, comic books, dissertations, cookbooks, training manuals, travel guides, yearbooks, photo books, calendars, music CDs, ringtones and other digital content—each month. The site says it logs monthly traffic of more than three million unique visitors.

It's not just authors who see a future in the on-demand universe. Recognizing there is a buck to be made in the self-publishing business, Amazon.com, the world's largest online book retailer, acquired the POD publishing company BookSurge in 2005. I guess

Amazon decided that if it could make money from readers it could make money from writers too. In fact, other POD companies have accused Amazon of predatory practices and the issue is now before the courts. You know that when an issue is before the courts then somebody somewhere believes they can make money!

How POD Works

Although it costs me nothing to sell books through Lulu, I did have to format my books and design my covers. I have some facility with Word and with a graphics program, so I was able to produce clean layouts and create functional covers. However, creating layouts and book covers could be onerous for some authors, so they might be better off with a POD company that provides such services or at least find a third party to prepare their books for publishing on Lulu.

Lulu allows authors to upload books and other digital content to its website, gives them a storefront address to sell from (such as www.lulu.com/paullima) and processes credit card orders. Lulu ships the books or makes Adobe PDF files and other digital content available for downloading. If you buy the electronic version of my books, the PDFs arrive almost instantly, without shipping charges, and you save money because Lulu does not have to print the books. Hard-copy books are printed on demand—one at time so Lulu does not have to carry inventory—and shipped to the buyer.

For hard copy books, Lulu sets the printing fee based on the number of pages and the page size. The author sets the retail price. Lulu takes a small percentage of the difference between the printing fee and the retail price and the author keeps the rest (known as the royalty). If I sell no books I earn no revenue, nor does Lulu. But I also never pay Lulu a cent unless I buy copies of my own books. When I buy copies of my books, I pay a wholesale fee, which consists of the printing price, a small mark-up and shipping. I can sell my books for any retail price I want.

As with Lulu, the POD company CreateSpace does not charge authors an up-front fee to get their books online. In addition, both Lulu and CreateSpace provide inventory-free, physical distribution of CDs and DVDs, as well as video downloads.

Most POD companies, such as Trafford Publishing, AuthorHouse, iUniverse, Xlibris, and others, charge an up-front fee for setting up books for publishing. This fee generally runs from $1,000 to $2,000, although you can find companies that charge less. POD companies that charge tend to give authors advice on how to format books. Some even help create book covers or offer editorial thoughts—services you can pay for, if you need them, through Lulu and other no-charge POD companies

Many POD companies place books with Amazon.com and other online retailers. This is a fee-base service that Lulu offers. However, I have opted not to pay for it because I drive traffic to my Lulu storefront through my website and blog (www.paullima.com/books and www.paullima.com/blog) and other online promotions. I let Lulu fulfill orders and I receive quarterly royalties.

If you are interested in online distribution through various Amazon outlets, and want to minimize the price you pay per book to have books printed (especially if you order small quantities), consider Lightning Source Inc. (LSI), a POD company owned by the book distributor Ingram. Books uploaded to LSI go into the Ingram book distribution catalogue and into the hands of online book retailers like Amazon, Barnes and Noble and W.H. Smith. If also want to distribute your book electronically, LSI can get your books into the hands of online e-book retailers. Many small publishers, or micro publishers, now use LSI to publish a range of authors who may not have mass appeal but who have found niche markets for their books.

For instance, *How to Write a Non-Fiction Book in 60 Days*, my book on writing non-fiction books, is published through Five Rivers Chapmanry, a micro publisher in Orangeville, Ontario. Five Rivers uses LSI so my book is not printed until orders are placed, saving onerous up-front printing fees and saving the publisher and retailers from having to carry inventory. The book is also available in electronic format (PDF file) through e-retailers like Books on Board and eChapterOne.

You need to know more about book layout and design when you use LSI than you do when you use many other POD companies, but if you are a do-it-yourself kind of person, LSI might be your best POD option. On the other hand, if you are not a do-it-yourself kind of person, you can always find someone to help you prepare your book for POD publication.

No Guarantees of Sales

Being a POD author using LSI, the Lulu distribution package or most any other POD company may guarantee your book a listing in many online retailers (not Chapters in Canada; for that you need to find an independent book distributor). However, a listing in an online retailer does not guarantee sales. Whether POD authors choose to sell through online retailers or from their web sites, marketing remains the responsibility of the author. Mind you, most authors who have had books published with traditional publishers in Canada, and for the most part in the U.S., will tell you that marketing pretty much remained their responsibility.

The question on the minds of most self-published authors is this: Can I sell my books? As of July 2009, I have sold well over 1,200 books. In addition, sales are trending up (most book sales trend down shortly after the initial launch euphoria abates).

I am not a famous author, but I am earning revenue from my book sales and I like the feeling of independence and control that POD self-publishing gives me, which is why I will continue to write books and promote them on my website and in various book-oriented e-mail lists and social media sites.

In addition, without the backing of a so-called "legitimate" publisher, I now sell my copywriting book to two university continuing education departments. My *Everything You Wanted To Know About Freelance Writing...* book is sold by another university continuing education department, and my *(re)Discover the Joy of Creative Writing* book is on the short list for a university creative writing course. My how-to book on writing media releases has been picked up by a do-it-yourself public relations website and my book on optimizing websites to boost search engine results is selling briskly to small businesses.

With Lulu's business model, I am running a virtual mail-order book business—but I don't process payments, ship books or keep a basement full of inventory.

Now, let's be honest. Most writers who self-publish will not be wildly successful, certainly not in *Harry Potter* or *The Da Vinci Code* terms, or even in terms of bestsellers (about 5,000 books). Most self-published fiction authors and poets publish for family and friends. They have no need for publishers or retailers; low-cost POD companies serve them well. However, many non-fiction authors sell books from websites or to complement talks and workshops, and POD—as thousands of authors have discovered—can be a very profitable niche market.

So at some point, if you feel you are ready to publish a novel, collection of short stories, a book of poetry or any other work, consider POD.

Note: Find out more about the author and his books below.

About the Author and His Books

Based in Toronto, Ontario (Canada), Paul Lima (www.paullima.com) has worked as a professional writer and writing and communications instructor for over 25 years. He has run a successful freelance writing, copywriting, corporate communications, business writing and media relations training business since 1988.

For corporate clients: Paul writes news releases, case studies, copy for direct-response brochures, sales letters, advertisements and other material.

For newspapers and magazines: Paul writes about small business and technology issues. His articles have appeared in the *Globe and Mail, Toronto Star, National Post, Backbone, Profit, CBC.ca* and many other publications.

Qualified educator: Paul presents in-class and online seminars on business writing, creative writing, search engine optimization and freelance writing.

Seminars, workshops and e-courses: Paul offers various seminars, workshops and e-courses on the business of freelance writing, writing for newspapers and magazines, and business writing. You can read more about his seminars, workshops and e-courses online at www.paullima.com/workshops and www.paullima.com/ecourses.

An English major from York University and a member of the Professional Writers Association of Canada, Paul has worked as an advertising copywriter, continuing education manager and magazine editor.

Paul is the author of 10 books and three short e-reports:

- *How to Write A Non-fiction Book in 60 Days*
- *Harness the Business Writing Process*
- *Everything You Wanted to Know About Freelance Writing…*
- *The Six-Figure Freelancer: How to Find, Price and Manage Corporate Writing Assignments*
- *Business of Freelance Writing: How to Develop Article Ideas and Sell Them to Newspapers and Magazines*
- *Copywriting That Works: Bright ideas to Help You Inform, Persuade, Motivate and Sell!*

- *How to Write Media Releases to Promote Your Business, Organization or Event*
- *Do you Know Where Your Website Ranks? How to Optimize Your Website for the Best Possible Search Engine Results*
- *Build A Better Business Foundation: Create a Business Vision, Write a Business Plan, Produce a Marketing Plan.*
- *(re)Discover the Joy of Creative Writing*
- *If You Don't Know Where You are Going, How are You Going to Get There? Business Vision Short eReport*
- *Building Your Business Plan and Your Marketing Plan: A Step-By-Step Guide to Planning and Promoting Your Business Short eReport*
- *Put Time On Your Side: Time Management Short eReport.*

All books are available at www.paullima.com/books.